AMUCK

Tales From a Hobby Farm

Sue Stein

2016
Dragonstone Press
Rosemount, Minnesota

Amuck: Tales From a Hobby Farm
Copyright © 2016 by Sue Stein

All rights reserved.
Printed in the United States of America
No part of this book may be used or reproduced in any manner whatsoever without written permission from the publisher except in the case of brief quotations embodied in critical articles and reviews.

ISBN: 978-0-692-59040-9
Library of Congress: 2015920078

Cover photo © Prahtnek Dreamstime.com
Loco the llama © Pat Haley, Prairie Lake Farm
All other photos © Sue Stein

Dragonstone Press
3820 120th St. W.
Rosemount, Minnesota 55068
www.dragonstonepress.com

To my friend, Connie Anderson

CONTENTS

Acknowledgments		i
Introduction		1
Chapter 1	Intro to Coyotes: 101	7
Chapter 2	Leaping Llamas	13
Chapter 3	Of Mice and Men	17
Chapter 4	Don't Mess With a Mini	21
Chapter 5	Dances With Deer	31
Chapter 6	Coyote Races	37
Chapter 7	Fifty Shades of Llama	43
Chapter 8	Sunny Goes Walkabout	49
Chapter 9	Tragedy Comes in Threes	55
Chapter 10	Rocky Raccoon	65
Chapter 11	Wing Swept	69
Chapter 12	Coyote Code of Conduct	73
Chapter 13	Midnight Riders	75
Chapter 14	Raccoon Olympics	81
Chapter 15	Misty Comes Calling	85
Chapter 16	Winner, Winner, Chicken Dinner	91
Chapter 17	The Great Mini Horse Escape	101
Chapter 18	The Turkey Trot	105
Chapter 19	Scrambled Eggs	111
Chapter 20	Muskrat Love	117
Chapter 21	The Bobcat Saga	123
Chapter 22	Roadkill Cafe	127
Chapter 23	A Rabid Coyote	131
Chapter 24	Sting Like A Bee	135
Afterword		139

Acknowledgments

That I emerged relatively unscathed from all the various (mis)adventures at my hobby farm with my sanity more or less intact is a testament to the help of my neighbors, John and Diane, and my friends, Connie Anderson and Tom Collopy. After each new traumatic happening, I fired off frantic emails to Connie and Tom, usually beginning with some variation of the words, "You will *never* believe what just happened..."

Connie commiserated with me, although I suspect she laughed when she read each email. Tom, ever pragmatic, invariably suggested that I invest in a shotgun, following up with, "You should just sell that place, and move to town where there's less wildlife."

I've thought about doing just that, until my attention is once again diverted to mopping up after the latest unfortunate incident. Here's to my friends—I'm glad I could make you laugh.

Introduction

Lions and tigers and bears and rabid bats, oh my! Well, okay—maybe there aren't any lions and tigers marauding through my property, but rabid bats and bears? Definitely.

I'm pretty sure there's been at least one big, furry teddy bear traipsing about near my house with nary a care in the world. My dogs could tell you all about it—if they could talk. And it wouldn't be the standard, "Woof-woof-rooo-wrrooof!" but instead would sound more along the lines of "Holy crap! What *is* that thing? It's a huge friggin' bear! Not gonna *think* of chasing that sucker." Anyway, that was my interpretation the night the dogs would not set foot off the front steps, but stared into the woods, growling, with hackles raised. If *they* were scared, I thought it might be a good idea if *I* was scared, too. We retreated with haste into the house, and I secured the deadbolt for good measure.

Before you decide I simply have a vivid imagination, there really *are* bears around here. I read about it in the local paper a week after our almost-encounter—a black bear was spotted in the regional park right across the road from me. It's not much of a stretch to think he gamboled across the road and hung out in the woods by my house. Not to mention my dogs have never reacted that way to any of the other wild critters around here—raccoons, foxes, coyotes, opossums, skunks, and whatever else is lurking out in the tall grass in the pasture—those are considered fair game. Nothing has ever scared my dogs, not until that night.

The rabid bat made its foray into my life on an idyllic summer afternoon as I happily lolled away the day in my hammock, reading a book. Out of the corner of my eye, I caught sight of something large and black passing up and over me. Looking up from my book I thought, *Man, that's a huge butterfly*, when it suddenly executed an aerial U-turn and flew back towards me. Then I identified it—the exposed needle-sharp fangs and beady black eyes were a big tip-off. It winged its way right at me. I rolled off the hammock and hit the ground running for the safety of the enclosed back porch, where I cowered in fear, looking out the windows in search of the bat. In my book, high noon on a sunny, hot summer day plus a flying bat equals rabid. For the next few days, I brought a broom whenever I went outside, fearfully scanning the sky in case it decided to come back.

My house is surrounded by ponds, and is tucked into the woods near the end of a gravel road. It's the home where I grew up, and this area hasn't changed much over the years. It's still rural, although other nearby areas have been built up into the requisite tiny cookie-cutter quadrants of suburbia. Progress, my ass.

Back when I owned a house in one of those same miniscule lots in a suburb, I tried to make it as wild as possible, to bring a little bit of the country into the city. It's built into my genetic code—I'll always be a country girl. When my parents passed away, I inherited the house and part of the land, while my brother got the other half. I was excited to move back to a more rural setting, and be more up-close-and-personal with the wildlife. I didn't realize until later just how up-close-and-personal it really would be.

Here in the country is where the deer and the buffalo play. Ahh, yes, my little slice of heaven is a veritable paradise. That's what I thought.

When I moved back to this property, I got two dogs to protect me in my new home out in the hinterland. Ask me how *that* worked out, and I'll tell you in a bit. Once I settled in, it took no time at all for me to accumulate a number of farm animals. After all, I live on what would be considered a hobby farm, so why not get some livestock? It seemed the thing to do.

First came a few chickens. However, it might have been a good idea to first have a coop to put them in upon arrival. A small oversight, easily rectified, to the eventual tune of several thousand dollars. When I build a coop, I don't go halfway, I go all in. The Coop de Ville came into existence, and the chickens lived in the lap of luxury.

Then, since the chickens were such a joy, I bought two miniature horses. I had wanted a regular-sized horse to ride on the trails in the nearby regional park, but for once I realized maybe I should start small and work my way up since I didn't know much about horses. At first it was fun. Now when people ask me what my mini horses, Misty and Sunny are good for, I say, "Eating hay and making manure." I conveniently leave out that they eat *lots* of hay—which leads to *lots* of manure.

To my dismay a few months after I got them, I realized mini horses would make a delectable repast for the hordes of coyotes infesting my property. I didn't make the connection until about eleven one morning, when I noticed a large coyote stalking the mini horses in the pasture. I watched as he made a circuit up and then down the trail, where he stopped and stared at something I couldn't see. This went on for at least five minutes until at last he left. The mini horses cautiously emerged from the corner of the fenced-in area where he had trapped them. I realized I needed to get a guard animal for them, since my dogs were hopeless in that respect. Soon after, a llama and several alpacas joined the burgeoning herd. Llamas are used as guard animals for livestock, especially sheep. I figured they would do just as well protecting my mini horses.

Well, I obviously hadn't thought all of this through because having animals, particularly in the cold and snowy winter, meant I had to feed them at least twice a day. At the time, my job required I be on the road by 5:30 a.m., which meant I had to schlep out to feed the animals even earlier. I had to walk several hundred feet in the pitch-black darkness with coyotes, along with the other unholy spawn lurking out there, watching my every move. I was scared to death, every single time. But my animals had to eat, and I had to conquer my craven nature and get the job done. It's no wonder my hair went prematurely grey.

The animals had to be fed twice a day no matter what; even when I was sicker than a dog and could barely move. One winter I caught a nasty stomach flu, so bad that I put my pillow and blankets on the floor of the hallway and slept there so I was close enough to crawl weakly into the bathroom. I lay there for three days, unable to eat and able to keep down only sips of water. Do you think I got a day off from taking care of the animals? No. I didn't. I remember shuffling out to feed them, bent over like a ninety-year-old woman, clutching the hay to my stomach, trying valiantly not to throw up. After what seemed like hours, I made it all the way to the fence where I made the massive mistake of energetically hurling the hay over the fence line. This motion made *me* immediately hurl over the fence as well. I collapsed on the snow, and lay there for twenty minutes in the fifteen-degree cold and wind before I had the strength to get upright and stagger back to the house. To their credit, the mini horses did gaze at me with mild concern while they munched.

I've been back here in the country thirteen years, and I still love being able to walk down to the dock on my back pond and watch the ducks and geese. I enjoy having coffee on the front step first thing in the morning, and being dive-bombed by hummingbirds demanding I fill their damn feeder, *now*. Eagles, hawks, and trumpeter swans have appeared in the sky over my house. I don't even mind the garter snakes that slither across the sidewalk right in front of me.

I've always loved animals—as long as they aren't stalking me from the underbrush.

Chapter 1

Intro to Coyotes: 101

The very first time I came face-to-face with a coyote, I went to investigate what was riling up my dogs. Shay, my Flat-Coated Retriever, had been barking at the edge of the yard, where a path leads down the hill to the back pond, while her daughter, Rosebud, ran back and forth like one of those games at the fair, where you shoot at the moving ducks.

I moseyed over and asked my dog what she thought was so darn interesting before I turned my attention to whatever it might be, and thought, *Uh oh...that's a coyote.*

Mr. Coyote and I were eye-to-eye, not ten feet apart. He stood on the path while I remained frozen at the edge of the woods. He took a moment or two to coolly look me over while I hyperventilated. And then, *Poof!* Gone like the wind. Those suckers can run faster than anything I've ever seen. Zero to sixty in 3.0 nanoseconds. No lie.

This was the first time I had far-too-intimate contact with a coyote. I've since gotten up-close-and-personal a few too many times for my own tastes, but what are you gonna do? Tell them to get lost? Actually, I do that now, every damn time I see or hear one of the furry bastards.

My neighbors (and thank god none of them are closer than a quarter mile and can't see my house) must find me highly amusing when I yell at the coyotes.

I used to like coyotes, and thought it was neat that they lived in my woods and pasture. I'm a real nature lover, and all the wild critters in my vicinity were reason to celebrate. That's what I used to think. Now I have a few more years of wild kingdom incursions under my belt, and many times I've felt as if I'm under siege. As a woman with no manly testosterone-charged backup in my life, I've had to learn how to defend my animals and myself.

At first I thought I'd carry a 12-gauge shotgun when I went out to feed my mini horses and chickens before the crack of dawn on workdays. I used to be a great shot. Not anymore. Now I would be lucky if I didn't shoot off my foot while I tried to juggle a shotgun, a chunk of hay, and the flashlight I used to scan around the yard, looking for any eyes watching me as I walked out to the horse pen. Try doing all those things when it's stinking twenty-below-zero and the snow is up to your knees. I settled instead on carrying an old wooden baseball bat as my weapon of choice for battle.

It's all about the body language anyway, when it comes to predator/prey relationships—and make no mistake, I considered myself firmly in the "prey" category. I felt like a walking, talking, hyperventilating first course as I trudged my way out day after day to feed the horses. I nervously scanned the flashlight back and forth across the yard, and even behind me periodically; you never know when those suckers are gonna sneak up on you. If I had ever actually seen any eyes reflected back in the light beam, I would have immediately ran back to the house, tripping over the baseball bat, hay, and flashlight. It wouldn't have been pretty. And it all would have been over anyway in a few nanoseconds, the time it would take Mr. Coyote to reach me as I floundered about in the snow, gibbering in fear.

I like to think the feral creatures in the woods were scared spitless by my utter ferocity and the Conan-the-Barbarian swagger of my body language as I walked. Although I was quaking in my vintage '70s-era moon boots, I tried my best to look like a hard-ass who was ready to rumble. At least I hoped I did. Predators can smell fear, I've heard. Maybe that's what made them stay clear. Too much fear smell must have overpowered them as they skulked in wait for their breakfast—me.

I've pretty much lost track of the numerous coyote sightings in my yard, but I remember with utter clarity the occasions when they went after my dogs, and I had to run off the coyotes. Yes, *me*, not the dogs.

Something is horribly wrong with the world when the dogs, which are ostensibly supposed to protect you, are in need of protection themselves. And these aren't cute little five-pound balls of fur—my dogs are 65–70 pounds. I know because I've had to carry them. Uphill. In flip-flops. But that's another story.

Why haven't any of my dogs—two Retriever mixes and a Smooth-Coated Collie—held their own against the coyotes? I used to think they could. Until the day I looked out my dining room window to the backyard and saw two coyotes with their jaws firmly locked on Shay's rear haunches, dragging her backwards towards the woods and certain death.

I ran outside and yelled, "Hey! Leave her alone!" They ignored me. I took a few more steps out in the yard, shook my fist in the air and yelled, "Hey, buttheads! I'm talking to *you*. Leave her alone!" This resulted in the coyotes taking a momentary break from dragging my dog. They looked at me with minor interest, and went right back to their hamstringing endeavors. I realized they didn't give a flying hoot about me, considering me no threat whatsoever. They were determined to kill my dog and eat her. I did what any other idiot would do—I ran towards them, screaming and yelling. It worked, and they took off.

That's when I snapped. Full-bore *snapped*. I grabbed my dogs, both thankfully okay, and put them inside the back porch, and then I hefted my trusty wooden baseball bat and went all Xena Warrior Princess, stalking out to where they had attacked Shay. I completely flipped out because I was *so* angry. And I wanted those furry bastards to know it.

This is where my neighbors' amusement factor I mentioned earlier comes into play.

At the top of my lungs, I yelled. I blustered. I bellowed. I told those mangy S.O.B.s *exactly* what I thought of them, and what I was going to do to them: "Show your faces, you worms! What, are you *afraid* of me? Get out here! I'm going to bash in your skulls!" And here I accentuated my words with the bat going *smash!* onto my cast-iron garden bench. Several times, making a resounding and very pleasing sound. "You hear that? That's your damn *heads* when I get ahold of you!"

By now I was probably foaming at the mouth. "Really? You're going to hide from me? I mean it, you pieces of crap! Get out here. I'm going to kill you! I'm gonna kill you *sooo* dead!" *Smash! Boom! Bang!* I slammed the bat onto more outdoor furniture. This continued for several more minutes until I ran out of swear words. Hey, what can I say—I can swear like a sailor when I'm scared to death, not to mention really angry. I'm sure the coyotes were lying flat to the ground in the underbrush, watching me, and marveling at the copious amounts of spittle flying from my mouth, and at the utter ballet of my body as I turned lightly on my heels and landed another smash of the bat, "That's your head, you jerks! Take that, will ya!"

All in all, a masterful performance. For my part, I offer the excuse that I was pissed, big time. I thought none of my neighbors had managed to hear me ranting—until I went to the nearby VFW about a week later and saw my neighbor Jeff. He lives about half a mile away, across two ponds and some woods. I was about to say hi to him, when he took a long, silent look at me, quickly turned, and walked in the other direction.

When I thought about it, I realized, to anyone simply hearing the words, it had sounded like a knockdown, drag-out domestic. He probably had thought I had been about to beat the living crap out of a boyfriend. I stood there alone in the VFW, snickering to myself. I didn't bother to correct his misapprehension. It's more fun that way. Keep 'em guessing, that's my motto.

Chapter 2

Leaping Llamas

If not for my miniature horses, Misty and Sunny, I wouldn't be wading through deer-tick infested pasture, and stumbling past vicious, attacking bramble bushes. Bad enough that it was 98 degrees in the shade, with more humidity than New Delhi. No, I had to be chasing down Loco the llama, who leaped the horse fence and made his getaway.

It all started with the coyotes. They were of the opinion horsemeat would be an utter delicacy, and they seemed to be planning an all-you-can-eat buffet, with my minis as the main course. They began stalking them, and I heard howling, yipping, and general salivating noises far too often that summer as the pack triangulated their positions and discussed strategy. I hopped into my Jeep more nights than I care to remember, and four-wheeled out to the pasture to check on poor Misty and Sunny.

I realized the coyotes meant business when, after they first attacked my dog Shay and I ran them off, they returned on two more occasions and attacked both Shay and Rosebud in broad daylight. I ran them off holding a baseball bat in a menacing manner, and screaming some rather choice words. I went to the gun club to practice shooting a 12-gauge shotgun. Considering how utterly uncoordinated I tend to be, I decided the gun wasn't going to be my first line of defense. And the baseball bat might make me feel brave, but I don't know how well I would fare brandishing a thirty-year-old wooden bat against a pack of slavering wild animals lusting for the kill. I'm sure they would consider me a singularly unappetizing hors d'oeuvre, and spit me out after the first bite.

That's where Loco entered the picture…or pasture.

I called the Minnesota DNR. I talked to trappers. I talked to the guy at the feed store. Everyone agreed. I needed a guard animal for my horses. I could get a llama or a guard dog, which, considering what the coyotes did to my so-called "guard dogs," didn't seem a good option. A friend, who has known me for far too long, related my dilemma to a co-worker who said, "Let me get this straight. She got dogs to protect her, and she ended up protecting the dogs." My friend replied, "Yup, that would be about right."

That meant getting a llama, because they like to kick coyote butt—sheep farmers use them to protect their flocks. My niece and I visited a local farm, and I decided that Loco the llama was the answer to my prayers. I told his owner I thought he'd make a great addition to my growing herd of farm animals. Too bad Loco didn't share the sentiment. Perhaps his name was an omen. But he was so darn cute, and furry, and so *big*. I could hardly wait for him to arrive at my hobby farm and meet the minis.

After one too many late-night coyote incursions, I stabled my minis in a hastily cobbled-together stall in a garage. They had room service several times a day, carrots and apples on request, and two fans blowing on them day and night. What wasn't to like? The minis had been cooling their hooves in the stall for a week or two, and were getting pretty antsy…or should I say, horsey?

The big day came, and Loco arrived. The owner led him out of the trailer. I looked up at him. And up again. Boy, he was much bigger than I remembered. We set him loose in his new home in the minis' pasture. He immediately melted inconspicuously into the sumac thicket, and peered out in what I can only describe as an expression of abject horror. Then we led Sunny and Misty up from the garage and set them loose. They really celebrated their freedom by galloping pell-mell, bucking indiscriminately, whinnying, and kicking as they raced past Loco in his hiding spot.

Loco the llama
Courtesy Pat Haley, Prairie Lake Farm

All too soon, in desperation, Loco leaped the fence and raced across the open pasture, heading for the neighbor's McMansion on the hill. Oh, dear god, how could I ever explain this to my well-heeled neighbors?

We ran after him in the stifling heat, yelling, "Loco! Loco!" Through the brambles a disembodied voice hollered, "He's over here." I pushed my way out of the thorn-encrusted brush to see a man and his cat, facing down the 450-pound llama nonchalantly standing by their garage. When Loco saw me, he darted off around the house and wended his way past rows of fabric-covered chairs and a flower-festooned arbor.

Loco had crashed a wedding rehearsal.

Sunny and Carbello

The wedding party feverishly snapped pictures as we cornered Loco. I vaguely remember saying, "Nice to meet you—I live down the hill."

After we led Loco back to my house, the owner and I looked at each other. Wordlessly he loaded him back into the trailer and drove away.

I got an alpaca instead because they are smaller, and more easily managed. His name was Carbello.

One day as I fed the mini horses and the alpaca their hay, a crashing and rustling sound came from the woods at the edge of their pasture. Carbello's long ears swiveled towards the disturbance, and he hooted out the alpaca version of a distress call. It sounded remarkably like a pheasant on steroids.

Carbello maintained a safe distance while managing to still look involved in the proceedings as Misty the mini horse charged off towards the incoming threat at full speed, ears back, and ready to kick some serious butt.

A wild turkey emerged. It took one look at the enraged horse bearing down on it like the Furies of Hell, and high-tailed it back into the woods.

Remind me again why I thought those horses needed "protection."

Chapter 3

Of Mice and Men

I seem to have no problem running full-bore at a growling coyote to protect my dogs, but if I see a mouse it brings me to my knees. Although I think mice are cute, I'm not sure what it is, but they make me scream in terror.

Case in point: A few minutes ago, I went out to feed the mini horses and chickens. I figured I should also check the level of propane left in the tank to make sure it didn't run out, leaving me with no heat in my house.

Sometime during the summer, I'd also checked the tank. A round metal piece on top covers the gauges and fittings. When I lifted the cover, these things began to dart around next to the gauges. It was so unexpected I screamed, and then noticed the bits of grey fur and leaves gathered into a pile.

It was a mouse nest, snugly set under the metal cover. And the *things* that were darting about?—they were itty-bitty baby mice. Their mom stood her ground and looked at me with her big brown eyes as if to plead for all of their lives, and the sanctity of their home.

I kept on screaming. It's incredible—a coyote doesn't bring about that knee-knocking terror like a wiggling little mouse does. And I like mice, just not unexpected mice.

Eventually, I told mama mouse that she'd have to find a new place to live, because it wasn't safe there. I cleared out all the nest materials with a stick. I felt like a jerk doing it, but the little family couldn't stay there. Mice teeth chewing on high-pressure gas hoses—not a good idea.

Fast forward to today. I walked out to the propane tank, and got ready to lift the metal cover, noting with idle interest some type of liquid had run from under the cover and down the side of the tank. Not to worry. I grasped the lip of the cover, lifted it, and let out a blood-curdling scream.

You'd really think the neighbors would have called the cops this time, because it sounded remarkably like a triple axe murder or something, but then, they do live next to me, so they pretty much ignore it. There were *more* mice—many, many more mice—and they were all grown up. And the nest? Many times bigger, and beautifully constructed of bits of fur, leaves, and twigs. And the liquid? Mouse pee, and lots of it.

Mice tumbled off the tank in all directions as they ran away from the source of the ear-piercing screams. Now it was down to just one mouse and me. Mama mouse stood her ground once again. She quivered in her little mouse boots, but she maintained steady eye contact with me, pleading once again for house and home. I finally stopped shrieking, and managed to speak calmly to her: "You have to move. You can't live here. It's a nice house and everything, and I can tell you did a lot of work on it. I'm sure it seems like a safe spot, but it isn't. When they come to deliver propane, they'll knock off your nest and kill you. You have to leave."

Her little whiskers wriggled, and her tiny front paws trembled, but she didn't move. I left the cover open so she understood it wasn't safe there anymore. I decided not to lean over her to eyeball the gauges in case she decided to leap up and attach herself to my jugular. I couldn't get close enough to see how much propane I had left, but I knew it wasn't much, so I went inside the house and turned down the heat. They'll deliver more propane tomorrow, and I hope the mice will have moved to a new toasty-warm nest.

Chapter 4

Don't Mess With A Mini

Carbello the alpaca had moved into the pasture with the mini horses several years before, shortly after the Loco the llama incident. He and the minis were best buddies, even when Carbello's libido overtook his better sense, and he mounted one or the other mini, and attempted sexual congress. Misty wouldn't put up with his shenanigans for long, but Sunny tolerated it, rolling her eyes in exasperation, and trotting forward in an attempt to dislodge her suitor. Carbello, in his position atop her rear end, usually held on for a minute or two. Long enough to do… well, I never watched long enough. Inter-species nookie was too disgusting looking. Yuck.

Other than his perverse tendencies, Carbello was the coolest guy ever. I absolutely loved him, and his big, soulful brown eyes. Alpacas aren't the cuddliest bunch, and he never let me pet him or get too close to him, but if I had a carrot or some lettuce, he was all too eager to eat right out of my hand. In the sweltering heat of summer, I'd fill his little plastic kiddie pool with ice cold water. He would climb into the pool, lay down with his belly underwater, and touch his nose to mine in thanks.

Alpacas are kind of like potato chips. You have one, and you want another, and another. And so I did—I got another alpaca.

A vet at the University of Minnesota large animal hospital, who specialized in alpacas, came to my hobby farm periodically to give Carbello his vaccinations, trim his toenails, and shave his coat in the summer.

After one such visit, she mentioned some alpaca breeders had left an alpaca at the animal hospital, and would I like to adopt him? For free? It took about three seconds for me to say, *yes!*

About a week later, I picked up the alpaca from the University animal hospital, making the drive to St. Paul during rush hour after work. I wasn't sure if he would fit in the back of my Jeep Wrangler after I removed the rear seat. When I arrived, the vets came out, checked the interior of the Jeep, and pronounced me good to go. They led out a handsome alpaca, and somehow managed to coax him up and into the back of the Jeep, where they tied his lead rope around the roll bar, leaving him enough room to lay down. He was a suri alpaca, with a long, silky white coat.

Lombardo enjoying his Jeep ride.

I was a bit nervous about the ride home—it normally takes over half an hour, and this was rush hour, so I knew I was possibly in for an entire nail-biting hour of excitement.

Driving along through the streets of St. Paul in heavy traffic, you can only imagine what the other drivers were thinking when they saw an alpaca looking at them though the back window of the Jeep. Lots of finger pointing, cell phones taking pictures, and huge smiles. It's not every day you see a farm animal while driving along in a major city. I felt a bit silly with an alpaca in the back of my Jeep, but what do you do? He only tried to get up once or twice, seriously freaking me out, but then both he and I realized the rope didn't have enough play in it. I remember thinking I might soon have an alpaca in my lap helping me drive, but that didn't happen. He was actually calmer than I was the whole drive.

We managed to get home in one piece, and I took a few moments before getting out of the Jeep to take pictures of him peeking his head between the seats. I wasn't sure how well he would behave if I tried to walk him all the way to the pasture, so I drove the Jeep through the yard, and backed it up so the tailgate was near the gate leading into the pasture.

Misty, Sunny, and Carbello all cantered down the hill to see what was up. I somehow extracted the new alpaca from the Jeep, and led him into the pasture. Everyone crowded around to check him out. His ears went back, Carbello's ears went back, and I knew it would take some time for them to acclimate to each other. I walked him around his new home to let him see where everything was, took off his halter, and let him go. He and Carbello had a number of dust-ups as they determined the pecking order, and yes, Carbello came out on top.

The vets told me my new alpaca didn't have a name, even though he was a few years old. I guess the previous owners had a large herd, and didn't consider them pets, and therefore didn't name them. At first, I took to calling him "New Guy," next I shortened it to "Guy," and considering his handsome good looks, a light bulb went on in my head: Guy…Guy Lombardo…Lombardo! And Lombardo it was.

The two alpacas and two minis settled into a peaceful coexistence. They all ate together where I tossed the hay over the fence. The two minis were always more pushy about the food. Misty particularly would shove her way in to get the tasty tidbits.

One day when I came home, I went to check on them, and from a distance I could tell something had happened to Lombardo. The right side of his face was all bloody. His eye was swollen shut, and blood was running down. I don't know exactly what happened, but I suspect Misty got mad at him while they were eating, and launched a kick that landed right on his eye.

This kind of emergency always seems to happen on a holiday weekend, and this was no exception. It was the Saturday of Labor Day weekend. I couldn't reach the vet at the University. I called all over to find a vet, any vet, who would be willing to come out to help him. A horse vet from an equine hospital about thirty miles away knew nothing whatsoever about alpacas, but she was willing to do what she could.

Carefully I put the halter over Lombardo's head, and led him out of the pasture so she could examine him. She didn't have a portable x-ray machine with her like many farm vets do, so she couldn't determine what damage had been done to his face and skull. The vet cleaned up Lombardo's face and bandaged his eye, and helped me put him into a makeshift stall I hurriedly cobbled together in my basement garage. I couldn't leave him outside—the coyotes would smell the blood, and he'd be their lunch. Additionally, flies would be all over him, which is not a good thing.

The vet gave me some ointment to put on his eye, and told me to change the bandages periodically. I spent the rest of the day researching on the Internet, trying to find someone who knew about another vet specializing in alpacas or llamas. I called a number of llama and alpaca breeders, and one, located about a hundred miles away on the Wisconsin side of the border, was home for the holiday weekend. She gave me tons of information and names of vets in my area. I ended up driving down to visit her a month later, and bought a llama from her. Like I said: Just like potato chips. You can't have just one (or two).

Poor Lombardo had to wait three more days, until the day after Labor Day, when I was able to get hold of a vet forty miles away who was willing to drive up to examine him. In the meantime, my always-helpful neighbor John and his wife came over to give me moral support. I was in way over my head, but I didn't know it. Lombardo was getting progressively weaker and more despondent. He wasn't able to stand anymore, and he could only lie in his straw bed. My hands were tied, and I was frantic—it was a holiday weekend, and unfortunately everything had to wait until Tuesday.

This new vet was an older man, a total no-nonsense, no-B.S. straight shooter. He unwrapped Lombardo's bandage, took one look at him and said, "In twenty-five years of being a vet, I have never seen anything this bad. You need to get him up to the University of Minnesota large animal hospital right away." Since he couldn't do anything for Lombardo, he left.

I wandered up to the pasture, and Sunny and Misty looked up at me from munching their hay. I really let Misty have it, because I knew she was the only one who would have kicked him. I yelled at her for some time. It was useless since she had probably forgotten the incident right after her hoof hit his face.

How was I going to get Lombardo up to the U? How could I get him into my Jeep? He was a limp noodle, and I knew I couldn't lift 175 pounds of dead weight up and into the Jeep.

Numb, and not knowing what to do, I turned to go back to the house. At the time, I had hired a service of really nice people who came weekly to pick up the dog poop in my yard. As I walked back to the house, the poop-scooper was walking up my front yard. She took one look at my face and said, "Oh my god. What's wrong?" That's when I burst into tears. I'd held it together the whole long, horrible weekend, trying to be strong, thinking I could handle this myself. Bullshit. I couldn't, and I really needed help.

Blubbering so badly I couldn't talk, I led her to the garage where Lombardo was laying in a heap in his straw. I explained I had to get him up to St. Paul to the University vets, and I had no way to do it. She didn't say a word. She dropped her poop scooper and ran to get her little Toyota hatchback. She backed it up to the garage and said, "Okay, let's get him in the back." I had to call my neighbor John to come help us, and it took all three of us to manage it. I don't know how we did it, or how Lombardo fit in such a small car. I put an old comforter on the ground, and we lifted him on top of it. Then we grabbed the edges of the comforter and dragged him to her car. Lombardo was too out of it to care. We heaved him up into the back of the car, and I wrapped the comforter under him so her car didn't get covered with blood. And we were off, driving like crazy toward the University.

Since this was where I had first picked up Lombardo, I knew where to go, and I ran into the back door to find a vet. The staff got the alpaca out of the car and onto a large, thick, hard sheet of black plastic with ropes on the sides. They told me I could ride along, and I sat down next to Lombardo to comfort him. They dragged the two of us through the halls and past stalls of horses, alpacas, dairy cows, and what-have-you. It would have been fun, except for the circumstances.

After the eye specialist examined him, they scheduled him for surgery. His eye had to be removed. After surgery he was a lot more comfortable—he must have had one heck of a headache before. They told me since alpacas are herd animals, it would be best if he had a buddy to hang out with him while he recovered, and this meant figuring out how to get Carbello to the University.

This time I called an old friend. I'd pretty much burned through everyone else with all the things that happen to me. I explained the situation, and asked if he would help. I'm sure he was thinking, *What am I getting myself into?* But he'd known me for years, so it was simply par for the course. We borrowed my brother's beat-up old Suburban, and pushed and prodded Carbello until he reluctantly got up and into the back. While my friend drove, I sat in the back seat and held my hand on Carbello's head because he was scared to death, poor guy.

Lombardo in his hospital stall after his eye was removed.

Lombardo was the perfect patient, and the vets and techs loved both him and Carbello. He got physical therapy to regain his strength—they strapped him into this medieval-torture-looking device on wheels, and slowly moved it down the halls so he could regain his leg strength. I tried to visit him every day after work. They told me he missed me when I wasn't able to come.

After a month, Lombardo came back home. He had lost about twenty-five pounds and still wasn't strong enough to be out in the pasture with the minis and the coyotes, so he and Carbello bunked in the garage stall. But the long hospital stay and convalescence took its toll. He developed a cough, and it turned into pneumonia. I called the no-

B.S. vet for advice, and drove the forty miles to his office to pick up a strong liquid antibiotic and syringes to inject it into Lombardo. But the antibiotic didn't help.

Very early before work one morning, I went out to feed and check on the two of them, only to find Lombardo lying unconscious in the straw. At first I though he was dead, and yelled his name. He raised his head a tiny bit. I ran back in the house, called in sick to work, telling them it was a "Family Emergency." Well, it was. I consider my pets like family, so it wasn't a lie.

Back outside, I fired up my Hyundai Sonata, drove it to the big garage door and opened the back door of the car. I knew I couldn't get him up into the back of my Jeep because it was too high, but was hoping I could get him into the back seat of a car. Once again I put him on top of a comforter, but this time I had to do it all myself. Who was I going to roust out of bed to help me at such an ungodly hour? Screw it! Xena Warrior Princess could do this herself.

I dragged the comforter to the open car door. Then I reached under Lombardo's chest to try to lift him. Alpacas have very deep chests, and I could barely get my arms around him. It took a couple of tries, but I heaved him upward until I got his front half up on to the seat. I ran to the opposite side of the car, opened the door, and crawled in to lift and drag him farther into the back seat. I went back and forth, until he was all the way in.

He had lost weight, but he still weighed at least 150 pounds. Five pounds more than I weighed. I still don't know how I did it. I prayed for the strength to do it, and suddenly I could.

On the half-hour drive to St. Paul, I reached back and held his foot the entire time, telling him to hold on, we'd be at the hospital soon. I stayed at the hospital with him the whole day as he periodically drifted off to sleep. He seemed like he was doing okay, so I went home. A few

Lombardo's last ride, in the back seat of my car.

hours later I received a frantic call from the vets saying Lombardo was having a really hard time breathing, there was no hope he would get better, he needed to be euthanized, and I needed to get back up there right away to be with him when they did it. Lombardo must have been holding it together for my sake while I was there, because they said he was now in agony.

Sitting on my front step in tears, I was wrestling with myself about euthanizing him, but after talking more with the vet, I made the hard decision, and drove back there. The vet had assured me Lombardo would be asleep the whole time because of the strong painkillers he had been given, which helped my squeamishness. I didn't want to have to look into his eyes, and tell him what I was going to do to him.

But wouldn't you know it, when I went to his stall he somehow heard me, and he lifted his head and looked right at me. I had to force myself to go in there and sit down in the straw next to him. I held his little foot again, and told him what we were going to do. And he somehow found the strength to roll up onto his stomach, lift his long neck, and kiss me right on the mouth—this, from a very standoffish alpaca who never acted like he cared whether I was there.

The vet came back with the injection, and I talked to Lombardo some more. Once again, he rolled up and kissed me on the mouth. All of us in the stall were in tears, including the vet. I held him while she administered the injection, and when it was over, gently laid his head back down in the straw.

It was after midnight when I got back home, so I waited until the morning to tell Carbello about his friend. And for once, he let me halter him without a struggle, and lead him up the yard to the pasture where his friends, the minis, waited. It was obvious they had really missed him, the way they nuzzled him, which helped me feel a little bit better.

I'd always been against euthanasia, thinking it wasn't my place to play God. But in this case, it was the right choice. It wasn't an easy choice, but it was Lombardo's choice all along. I didn't realize it until he thanked me with his kisses.

Chapter 5

Dances With Deer

The elusive and timid whitetail deer: known for being such quiet, gentle creatures of the forest, and quick to bound gracefully away in escape at the first hint of danger.

Right. Maybe the deer in my neck of the woods didn't get that memo.

Several years ago the dogs and I were inspecting the progress of my so-called vegetable garden, located in the front forty of my expansive yard. While examining the bite marks on a decapitated green bean plant, I noticed Shay and Rosebud a few feet away, at the edge of the woods, busily sniffing at something. Since there was no point in my looking at the rest of my decimated bean plants, I dusted the dirt off my knees, and walked over to the dogs.

They totally ignored me, even when I bent down next to them and asked, "What's so interesting, girls?" It was early summer, so the wild blackberries and assorted sticker bushes on the edge of the woods were fully leafed out, and I couldn't see much of anything in that mess.

I stood back up, about to turn away, when it happened.

Rosebud

A small brown-and-white creature shot straight up from where it had been concealed amongst the leaf litter under the bushes. It launched itself upwards with pinpoint accuracy until it hit me square in the center of the chest. My arms reflexively grabbed for it as it repeatedly head-butted me.

Looking down, I saw a fawn in my arms, only a day or two old.

In my confusion prior to realizing what manner of creature had attacked me, I dropped it, and it ran off into the woods, bleating as it ran. Back and forth it raced, crying for its mommy. Of course, I felt horrible about dropping the poor infant, and I called out, "I'm sorry! I didn't mean to drop you!" as it crashed through the underbrush.

The dogs had remained remarkably calm throughout this whole ordeal, sitting by my side and listening as the fawn raced around. I have no idea why it leaped at me; was it, even at that tender age, trying to protect itself? It never did come back out, and I'm hoping its mom later found it.

Each summer, the mother deer and their fawns wander through my yard, nibbling on delicacies such as my hosta plants and the roses—in short, everything that is edible, and everything I don't want them to eat. Sometimes twins are born, and I get to watch the babies as they grow into their teenage years—when it becomes hard to tell all of them apart.

Certain deer recognize me and, in their passage through my yard, they stand and stare at me before moving on. It's mostly the bucks that do that, for whatever reason.

Years ago, as a teenager living at this house with my parents, I used to like to go out to the pasture in the fall to do my homework. I'm not sure why, other than on a beautiful fall day, there was no place I'd rather be than out in the middle of nature. One day I sat cross-legged in the grass with my notebook across my knees, and my nose buried in my textbook.

Shay

The day was sunny and mild, with a light breeze blowing my hair about my face. Everything was completely quiet, but some inner sense made me look up. Standing right in front of me, perhaps ten feet away, was a huge buck—eight-pointer, ten-pointer, who was counting? His head was bent down towards me, and he was staring with curiosity right into my eyes.

He was absolutely gorgeous. I didn't have time to panic, even though it was rutting season, and a testosterone-charged buck is nothing to mess with. Even back then, I always talked to the animals, and so I said hello to him. I was starting to realize it might not be such a great idea for me to be sitting in such a defenseless position, particularly because I didn't know what he might be capable of doing.

Glancing down at the ground for just a moment, I wondered what I should do. When I looked up, he had vanished, with absolutely no sound. It was uncanny. A bit shaken, I dusted the grass off me as I stood up, looking around for him, but he was gone. Back at the house I told my family what had happened, but of course, they didn't believe me.

Talking about testosterone-charged bucks reminds me of another recent incident. Another fall day in the late afternoon, the dogs and I were sitting on the front steps, enjoying the day. Breezy, the Smooth-Coated Collie who moved in shortly before Shay died, usually notices everything going on around her, and she's the first to leap into enthusiastic pursuit.

So I was a bit surprised when I noticed the ten-pointer moseying down the driveway, his head to the ground, snuffling for the scent of his soon-to-be conquest. I looked over at Breezy, and she hadn't a clue he was there. I watched the buck zigzagging his way closer. He was in full rut, and nothing else mattered but finding a girl deer. He, too, had no idea we were there.

He soon made his way behind the detached garage, where I'm sure the penned-in mini horses were watching his passage with interest. He emerged from behind the garage, and was now in the yard to the side of the house, nose still down, snuffling loudly. He paused for a moment as it registered in his sex-addled brain just where he was standing. He raised his head, looked right at us, and froze in place as he put the pieces together: two dogs, one human. Hunting season. *Uh, oh.*

That's when Breezy finally noticed him. She was frozen in place also, as she couldn't believe what she was seeing—one of those fun-to-chase big, brown creatures was standing *right there*. The chase was on. The buck dug his back feet into the dirt, pushed off, and bounded away, making for the woods. Breezy practically left flames in the grass as she streaked off after him. He made it to safety, of course. And Breezy came back after some time, sides heaving as she panted from her exertions, with a huge smile.

The deer eat everything around my house, especially in the winter when the snow is deep and food is scarce. It's not unusual to step outside and see fresh deer prints on the sidewalk right next to my house. They eat the evergreens, they eat the shrubs, I've even caught them eating out of the birdfeeder in the middle of the day.

Looking out the living room window one afternoon, I saw three does clustered around the birdfeeder by the sidewalk. One of the female deer used her nose to nudge the birdfeeder into swinging on its hook, thereby allowing the seed to fall onto the ground where they all could partake of the succulent morsels.

I watched them through the window for at least fifteen minutes. They knew I was there, and looked up periodically, with absolutely no concern. Perhaps they thought I put out the buffet especially for them.

Last winter was particularly brutal here in Minnesota—it hit twenty-below-zero on several nights, the snow just kept coming (it snowed in May, for heaven's sake!), and it was a rough winter for any animals living outside.

Groups of three to five deer visited my house at night looking for something to eat. Breezy alerted me with her barking, and when I looked outside I could just make them out in the wan moonlight. They were struggling through the deep snow, which was so deep they were unable to dig down for acorns or grass to eat.

Of course I had to do something to help. The next day, I went to the feed store in town and asked them what I could buy to feed the deer. Deer chow, that's what. I had no idea things like that existed. I bought a fifty-pound bag and, that afternoon, scooped some into an ice cream bucket which I placed in the backyard about twenty feet from the house.

Like clockwork, the deer arrived around ten that evening. This time it was three bucks, their antlers still attached in late February. The smallest sniffed out the bucket of deer chow first. He got in a couple of bites before the biggest buck shouldered him out of the way and devoured the rest of the food. The other two waited submissively but only a few bites remained, scattered on the snow.

The next night, I put out three buckets of chow, thinking that meant everyone would be able to eat. Wrong. The same group returned, and the big buck again hogged all the food. I had placed the buckets too close together, and he was able to guard all three buckets, dishing out shoves to his buddies when they got too close.

Okay. Two can play at that game. The next night, I put the three buckets ten feet from each other, which worked better. Try and guard that, buddy! I kept watch, and all of the deer were able to eat. The three gobbled down all the food, upending the buckets, and pushing them with their noses to find any remaining bits of food. They left, and soon five more deer wandered in from the woods and up to the food buckets. Word must have gotten out—free food at Sue's place. So the next night, I put out five buckets.

Until the snow melted, a revolving door of deer visited my backyard for the all-you-can-eat buffet.

Chapter 6

Coyote Races

In the morning when the weather is nice, I like to sit on the front steps with my dogs while savoring a strong cup of coffee. I groggily sip at the mug of steaming Joe, and try to wake up.

Most mornings it's fairly relaxing, communing with nature and sitting in quiet companionship with my two dogs. *Most* mornings. Some mornings, though, the stuff hits the fan in spectacular fashion before I've had the chance to come completely awake. Two mornings in particular come to mind, and they both involve the usual suspects: my dogs, and coyotes.

The first event involved my Smooth-Coated Collie, Breezy, and Mr. Big-Ass Coyote. I had barely sat down on the front step at 7:00 a.m. and taken a sip from my mug of the life-giving elixir when Breezy bolted off across the yard. I saw the coyote standing in the yard by the woods where the land takes a precipitous drop down to one of the ponds. Breezy high-tailed it straight at him, and the chase was on. Mr. Coyote streaked like a missile down the hill, with Breezy after him. I lost sight of both of them as I ran over to where I'd last seen them.

I could follow the progress of the chase by the crashing sounds

Breezy keeping a watchful eye for furry intruders.

coming from the thick underbrush. Breezy was hot on his tail. What I most worried about was what would happen when she caught up with him.

Breezy is the only one of my dogs that has never been chewed on by coyotes. Both Shay and Rosebud had been attacked in previous years. Unfortunately, my trusty baseball bat was still in the house, so I reached down to the ground and grabbed the first blunt instrument I could locate: a small oak branch. I launched myself in swift pursuit. Who am I kidding here? More like lumbering than swift, and I stayed on the lawn rather than entering the woods because I was barefoot.

Breezy and the coyote raced along the edge of the pond and up to the driveway, which is about a tenth of a mile long. I ran as fast as I could without having a coronary. The coyote and my dog popped out of the woods and onto the driveway as I gasped my way along. They were in a face-off about twenty-five feet apart, thankfully with the dog closer to me.

Standing in solidarity with Breezy, I menacingly waved my branch at the coyote. Right about then I realized I was wielding a *rotten* oak branch because, in mid-wave, half of it fell off onto the ground. Three times the coyote turned to come back towards us, and three times I yelled and waved my killer branch stub at him, which didn't dissuade

Misty on the loose in the front yard with Breezy. Both coyote incidents took place where the driveway heads uphill.

his progress in the least. It's funny how much time you have to think in situations like this. In fact, you only have seconds to process everything and act, but for some reason, you can think about your possible demise in its many possible permutations for what seems like hours.

My lightning-quick thought processes presented me with the sure knowledge that I would be toast if I turned tail and ran. Coyote toast. Before I could think things through, my reptilian caveman brain took over, and I ran right at the coyote, waving my rotten piece of oak, yelling at the top of my lungs. It watched me for a moment or two, before racing off in the other direction.

After all of my exertions, I was gasping for breath and felt like I was going to collapse. I grabbed Breezy by the collar and dragged her back to the house, all the while trying to keep my warrior body language intact in case the coyote was watching for any sign of weakness.

The second early-morning scenario started off remarkably like the one above. I had just staggered out to sit on the step with my coffee. I wasn't capable of thinking straight, since I hadn't even taken a sip.

This coyote was bigger than the other one. He was right by my house, and lured Breezy into the woods by the same pond. They raced along exactly like the last time in the sticker-bush infested woods. I was relegated to running up the gravel driveway in my jammies and bare feet, yelling "Breezy! Breezy! Get your butt back here!" I didn't feel the rocks digging into my feet as I raced up the drive. I ran full-out the whole way, which I don't do, *ever*, and then that monster coyote came out of the woods and stood right in the middle of the driveway, bold as day. He flicked his gaze to me, and our eyes locked for a brief moment. He quickly decided I was a non-entity in this fight, and turned his attention back to Breezy.

It was a good thing I'd put on Breezy's Invisible Fence collar, because it meant she couldn't venture any further up the driveway without getting a shock from the collar. As it was, the coyote was within twenty feet of us—way too close in my book—or in any book, for that matter. I did all the things I normally do to make the big bad coyote run away, like yell and wave my arms. Nothing. This one wasn't going to be dissuaded. He wanted a piece of Breezy, and nothing was going to get in his way—not even me.

The coyote's ears were back, his teeth were bared, and his body was turned sideways as he sidled towards us. He was probably growling too, but my heart was hammering too loud for me to know. I was more scared than I think I've ever been, because this sucker meant business. I looked at Breezy, and she seemed perplexed because of the way the coyote was acting. She thought it would run off because she had chased it. I didn't have a stick this time, so I waved my arms and yelled. He kept coming at us. My inner caveman again took over, and I charged at him, and growled as loudly and fiercely as I could. I acted like I was a rabid, crazy lunatic. I pretty much was, to do something that stupid. But it worked. He decided I was an absolute freakin' nutcase, and he didn't want to stick around to see what would happen if I reached him. He was gone like a shot up the driveway and into the woods.

He was so pissed he started yipping and howling from where he was hiding in the woods—I could hear how mad he was in his voice. But I was *more* pissed. I stood in the center of the driveway, shook my fist above my head, and started yelling at it. It howled some more, and I was so angry I howled right back. And I yelled some more: "Oh yeah, you piece of crap? Come here and say that!" And I interspersed far more graphic language in amongst my howls and yips. I figured I would talk to him in his own language. Okay, so maybe coyotes don't have quite the wide-ranging graphic vocabulary I do, but I'm sure they know what it means. It's all about your tone of voice, in my opinion.

Sometimes I surprise myself. Not too many middle-aged women would take on a coyote, although I think most of those mangy bastards—coyotes, not middle-aged women—know I would do my best to rip them to pieces in hand-to-snout combat if they tried anything.

Ah yes, my neighbors certainly had a great audio show that morning. Too bad they couldn't witness the visual.

Chapter 7

Fifty Shades of Llama

Shortly after Lombardo died, Churchill, the llama, moved in with Carbello and the mini horses. Churchie, who was only six months old, had never been away from his mother, and he took to suckling Misty and Sunny. I have no idea what they thought of this, but they let him do it.

I bought him from the llama breeder who'd helped me out over the phone when Lombardo first got hurt over the Labor Day weekend. Her farm was down by Winona, on the Wisconsin side of the Mississippi River. One day when Lombardo was still in the large animal hospital, I took a day off from visiting him and drove down to meet her and learn more about llamas. This breeder had every size and shape of llama you could envision, and we walked out to meet them in the pasture. I updated her on Lombardo, and told her I thought a llama might be a good idea for predator control to protect the mini horses and alpacas.

We sat on her porch, coffee in hand, and talked. I watched several massive male llamas graze in her yard, tethered to tires just heavy enough so they could move about the yard, but not get any escape ideas. She took me into a shed to instruct me on how to give the monthly deworming injections to my alpacas, rather than paying a vet. She brought a female llama into the shed and demonstrated, and then she led in another llama for me to try it.

I'm not squeamish around needles, but because llama skin is so tight and thick, I really had to struggle to get the needle in while the llama moved around. It was kind of gross. Since I had a hard time juggling the needle and the llama at the same time, the breeder showed me how to pin the llama against the side of the stall with my body, holding one arm around the base of its long neck to keep it still while injecting the dewormer with my other hand. Good lord, I can't walk and chew gum at the same time, and she expected me to accomplish this monumental task?

The breeder took the llama back outside after I finally managed to get the needle in and inject it. Soon she came back in leading the biggest llama I've ever seen—bigger than Loco the Llama, he of wedding rehearsal-crashing fame. She told me, "If you can handle this big boy, you can do anything." She explained that body language is key when working with llamas and alpacas. You have to project that you're the one in charge—and have bigger cojones. Considering the fact my animals shamelessly manipulate me, I wasn't sure if I was up to the task.

Big Damn Llama (BDL) looked down at me with contempt, and curled his lip. He didn't spit at me, though. I filled the needle with the solution, and gritted my teeth for the next step. I walked up to BDL and pushed him toward the wall to hold him there. He pushed back. I tried again, same thing. I went for it—I body slammed that 500-pound behemoth, and got him right where I wanted him. I snaked my arm around his neck, and he was like a bucking bronco. But I held on, and I won. I held him up tight

Baby Churchill safe inside a pen on his first day here, with Carbello watching his every move.

against the wall, rammed the needle in and injected the dewormer. I was exhilarated that he didn't kill me dead. Yay, me.

After undergoing this adventure, I'm not sure why, but I decided to buy a llama from her. After having faced my possibly incipient demise by BDL, I still bought one. Fully aware of my llama-related ineptitude, she selected a toddler llama, and Churchill arrived at my house a few weeks later, right after Lombardo died.

Churchie was soooo cute, a real doll with his big soulful brown eyes, dark brown coat, and about the size of full-grown Carbello. Carbello didn't share my sentiments, unfortunately, and he made life rough for the tot for several weeks. Finally things settled down and Carbello, Misty, Sunny, and Churchill coexisted in relative peace.

When spring finally came around, Churchie was almost full-grown. It was time to clean up the pasture of all the fresh manure,

Baby Churchill practicing his moves on an annoyed Misty.

since manure draws in flies—lots of flies. I trundled the heavy old wheelbarrow out there and started shoveling. Trip after trip I made with that stuff out of the pasture and off to another location. Good exercise, but not at all fun.

I'd returned for another pungent load, and pushed the wheelbarrow up the hill past where all of the animals were munching hay. I bent over, scooped up a shovelful, and slung it into the wheelbarrow. Scoop, sling, scoop, sling…I was getting into a good rhythm and feeling like maybe I'd be done before Christmas, when I suddenly got an eerie feeling I was being watched.

Turning my head, I saw Churchill had crept up silently to within feet of me, and he was eyeing my derriere, which was at the moment conveniently pointed right at him. I stood up fast, and spun to face him. He had unbridled lust in his eyes. I raised the shovel between us, "You'd better not be thinking what I think you're thinking!" I slowly backed away, right into the wheelbarrow full of manure.

Misty and Sunny turned their heads to watch the drama unfold while continuing to munch on their hay. Carbello completely ignored us because he thought Churchill was a fool anyway. Churchie crept forward a few paces, craning his serpentine neck to try and cop another eyeful of my ass-ets.

Churchill as an adult.

"Oh, no. Not a step closer, buddy!" I held the shovel in a defensive position in front of me. He was fully aware I wasn't a llama—but he just didn't care. Any port in a storm, as they say.

We stood facing each other in an eye-to-eye standoff. After several tense minutes, he lost interest and wandered back to the pile of hay where Misty nipped at his legs. I tossed the shovel in the wheelbarrow and got out of there. After that, I made sure to never again offer my backside to his lecherous gaze. However, the breeder did tell me it was all about body language, didn't she? And what screams, *Come and get me, big boy!* to a male llama louder than an outthrust behind? It's not every day you have a 400-pound llama looking for a bit of love—a tumble in the hay, so to speak.

Chapter 8

Sunny Goes Walkabout

My new part-time job at Target started at 8:30 a.m, and like usual, I was already running late. Just after eight, I went out to feed the animals. Llama—check. Alpacas—check. Two mini horses, oops, I saw only one. Where's the other damn mini horse?

The gate was chained and padlocked, and of course I had lost the key, so I climbed up and over the gate and hopped down. As I ran around the pasture looking for Sunny, I didn't see any suspicious piles of blood or guts, which meant the coyotes didn't get her. Plus they wouldn't have been able to drag the rest of her carcass out of there. She's too fat.

Rushing back to the house, I grabbed a halter and lead rope. I jumped in my car and sped off to see if she was on the road. I kept trying to call Target to tell them what was going on, and that I would be late, but each time the cell phone said the number was disconnected. When I checked, I was dialing the right number. It was like the Twilight Zone, much like the rest of my life.

At the end of my driveway, I got out to look for hoof prints in the dirt. None. I didn't know what to do, and I was frantic anyway from being late to my new job. I decided, *what the heck,* and called the non-emergency line at the police department and asked if anyone had reported seeing a mini horse. Yes, I called the police because I was worried about Sunny getting hit by a car, but more worried about the people in the car getting hurt from hitting her. It was the only decision I felt I could make at that moment.

The police told me to wait in my car on the road. A nice female officer arrived, and told me she has had to herd full-size horses with her squad car out on the highway. She was totally calm, like it was any other workday. I meanwhile, was still frantic, telling her it was the first few days on my new job, and I couldn't get hold of them to let them know why I wasn't there.

She dialed the number on her phone as she sat in her car, and it went right through. I stared at her in wonder as she handed me the phone so I could tell the store manager what was going on. "Uh, I know this sounds weird, but, ummm…I'm late because my mini horse escaped, and now the, uh, the police are helping me…ummm…catch her…" Can you imagine how ridiculous that sounded? *I* thought it sounded suspect—and *I* was the one telling it.

As I handed the phone back to the officer, she told me she'd keep looking on the road, and would also check with the county to see if Sunny had gone into the regional park right across the road from me, which is thousands of acres. She gave me her cell number and told me to call her if I needed more help. When she drove off, I decided to drive into my brother's driveway since his property adjoins mine through the pasture.

And there was Sunny, calmly munching grass in front of his house. My brother was up at the cabin with his family, and wasn't around to witness the debacle.

Parking my car, I got out and took three steps toward her, but she ran the other direction. This went on for some time until I was thoroughly sick of it. I considered calling my neighbor, John, but I didn't think he'd be home, and he's bailed me out of so many predicaments I hesitated to bother him again. If there had been anyone else for me to call, I absolutely would have—so feeling very foolish, I called the officer's cell phone to see if she could come back and help me.

Sunny munching on my brother's succulent lawn.

After we chased Sunny around the house for forty-five minutes, the officer caught her, and I put the halter on Sunny. The officer probably thought the problem was solved, and she could get back to doing something else, like a *real* crime or a *real* emergency. Wrong. There was still the problem of how to get the horse back *into* the pasture since the gate was padlocked and I had lost the key.

I led Sunny back through the pasture to her pen, with the squad car four-wheeling behind, lurching and bouncing over gopher mounds. Imagine what it looked like to the people living in the McMansion on the hill, seeing a police car driving through the pasture below. They had a perfect panoramic view of the proceedings. I'm sure they were still reeling from the escaped llama performance of a few years prior.

Since using the gate was out of the question, the two of us had to try to shove a 250-pound miniature horse under the electric fence wire. Didn't work. Sunny got herself out that way, but she refused to go back in. It was like trying to force yourself into the jeans you wore in high school. Ain't gonna happen. Carrot bribes offered from inside the fence didn't help to lure her. All I could think of as we were pushing the mini horse towards the fence were the stories the cops were going to tell each other about this whole boondoggle. Even now I cringe to think about it.

The officer got a call on her radio about a medical emergency. I heard the words, "respiratory arrest" and "seven-year-old boy." I could tell by the sick-to-her-stomach look on her face she knew exactly who it was. I stopped trying to shove Sunny and said to her, "That's way more important than this. I'll figure something out. You need to go there. This doesn't matter at all. Thank you for helping me."

She drove the squad car down the hill towards my house, through the front yard, and off she went, lights flashing, and sirens blaring. I led Sunny down to the garage, gave her some hay, and left her in there while I tried to figure out what to do.

In the basement, I rounded up some tools and went back out to the pasture. No way was I going to be able to remove the padlocked chain. I pondered the problem a while, and proceeded to try and take the entire gate apart. No go. My handyman skills are rudimentary at best. They tend towards pointing the blunt end of the hammer at the nail and yelling, "Ouch! Shit that hurts!"

Finally I gave in and called my neighbor, John, who has horses—the one I didn't want to call because he always bails me out. He was able to get the chain off the gate somehow, and he led Sunny out of the garage, up to the pasture, and shoved her in. By that time, I was nearly curled into a fetal position, so it was good that he took over. He knows how to get horses to do what he wants. It was best he was there, because horses know how to get me to do what they want.

How did Sunny get out? She had figured out the battery on the fence charger was dead, and the fence wire wouldn't zap her if she went under it. I'm not sure why Misty didn't escape too, considering she had done the majority of the previous jailbreaks. Driving my Jeep up there, I opened the hood and hooked the Jeep battery up to the fence charger to electrify the wires while I brought the other battery to the house to recharge it.

After the three hours it took to get that horse back in the pen, I didn't bother to go to my job, since the shift would have been over by the time I got there. Sunny was still in her pasture the next morning, but she wasn't in any mood to talk to me. After John and I got her back in the pasture, she had wandered off to the corner of the fence and looked wistfully in the direction of the succulent grass at my brother's house.

Believe me, that day went to hell in a handbasket, I think I drank half a bottle of wine that night. But the worst part—in the local paper the next week was an obituary of a seven-year-old boy. And all I could think of was that he might have lived if the police officer had been closer to town, and had gotten to him sooner, instead of helping me. I'll never know for sure, but it still brings tears to my eyes thinking about it.

Chapter 9

Tragedy Comes in Threes

Maybe I should have stuck with having only the one alpaca, Carbello, along with my mini horses, because after I added to the herd, one tragedy after another happened. I'd had Carbello for a couple of years before I got Lombardo as a companion for him. That went fine for about a year, until Misty kicked Lombardo's eye, and shortly afterwards he died. Churchill, the llama, joined the herd right after Lombardo died. About a year later, I made the mistake of visiting a local alpaca breeder, and she sold me Ace, a gorgeous black suri alpaca.

Ace was a few bricks short of a full load, but he got along okay with the other boys, Carbello and Churchill. They'd come bounding down the hill together when they saw me coming their way with hay. I took to calling them the Three Caballeros. Misty and Sunny shook their heads in bemusement, wondering why I didn't get another mini horse instead of another one of those weird-looking animals.

Ace had been here only a few months, and it was another one of those hot, unbearably humid summer days, like being in a rotisserie oven. I'd gone to town to run errands, and when I came back a few hours later, I went to check on them. Everyone except Ace was present and accounted for, eating grass near the fence. I climbed over the gate to see where he was, because he never missed a meal. He was dead under a tree, having somehow hung himself. A vine had wrapped around his neck several times, leaving his head suspended a few inches above the ground, and another vine was down his throat.

When I checked to see if there were any signs of life, there were none; he was dead as a doornail. I ran back to the house to get something to cut the vine, sobbing all the way. On my way back into the pasture, I said to the rest of the animals, "Ace is dead. He's fricking *dead*. What the hell am I going to do?" They followed me back to where Ace lay. Carbello sniffed at him. I used the scissors to cut the vine away, and Ace's head dropped with a thunk to the earth. If that wasn't gross enough, I had to pull the vine out of his throat, and when the trapped air was released, it sounded like a huge sigh.

The flies were already circling, so I couldn't leave him lying there in the hot sun. I grabbed his back legs, and dragged his 200-pound body through the dirt all the way to their three-sided shed, a.k.a. the mini mansion, sweating the whole way. I dragged him inside out of the sun, and then I bent over with my hands on my knees to try to catch my breath, and to cry some more. Churchill and Carbello came inside with me to pay their last respects to their buddy, which made me cry even more. I pulled my cell phone out of my pocket and called my neighbor who always bails me out. He wasn't home. It was the weekend, and he and his wife must have been busy. I left a totally incoherent message, asking if he could bring his skid loader down and bury Ace, my dead alpaca.

Running back to the house, I found the phone number of another neighbor who I knew owned a skid loader. He wasn't home either, and I left another sob-filled message. When he called back within the hour,

Ace munching on hay several
weeks prior to his untimely demise.

I explained what happened, and that I didn't know what to do with my dead alpaca—and could he come bury him?

Soon enough I heard his Bobcat coming down my driveway. He followed behind in the Bobcat as I led him to the pasture and up to the mini mansion. Carbello was standing guard inside, forlornly looking out the window. He'd lost another friend, and he was grieving.

The neighbor and I grabbed onto opposite ends, and hauled Ace onto the bucket of the Bobcat. He drove out to another part of my property, and dug a deep hole to bury Ace.

First Lombardo, then Ace. What was next? Carbello, sweet, gentle Carbello was the next one to bite the dust. It took a couple of years, but the Grim Reaper had him in his sights. He'd been getting skinnier, and I had an appointment set up for the vet to come examine him. The vet had to cancel, and could come a week later—but a week was too late for Carbello.

Carbello, the coolest guy ever.

If summers are unbearably hot and miserable in Minnesota, the winters are worse. Twenty below zero and thirty-mile-an-hour winds make for a character-building walk out to feed the animals twice a day. You'd think alpacas would be able to handle the cold, but I ended up buying them coats (yes, they do sell coats specifically for alpacas) to help them bear the icy cold. Misty and Sunny were jealous because, why didn't I get them coats? So, I bought fleece fabric and Velcro, and jury-rigged a couple of coats for the minis. Even with their haute-couture coats, it was still damn cold out there, and they spent most of their time inside the mini mansion where the south sun angled in and warmed them. Of course, this meant I had to slog up through the snow and wind to deliver their hay inside the mini mansion. I'm dumb that way. I'm pretty sure I'm supposed to train the animals, but in truth, they train me.

It was a brutal winter, extremely cold, with snow up to my thighs. I'd blazed a narrow trail from the house all the way to the pasture, and then up the hill to the mini mansion—probably the distance of a football field—we're talking a really difficult trip twice a day to feed my animals.

Carbello had a hard time getting up one morning, and I was really worried about him, but I couldn't get the vet out any sooner. I prayed for the best. First thing the next morning I went out in my jammies, moon boots, and parka to check on him. The minis poked their heads out of the mini mansion, but no Churchill, and no Carbello.

Curled up in the corner, with Churchill guarding his body, Carbello had died sometime in the night. A number of thoughts ran through my mind: *Not again! Not another dead animal.* And one thought in particular, *Please, not Carbello.* But there he was, dead, right in front of me Just so you know, it's no fun crying in twenty-below weather, because the tears freeze to your face and eyelashes like little icicles. I knelt down next to him in the straw and sobbed, grieving for the coolest guy ever.

Once again, I had to figure out what to do. I couldn't leave him there; he would end up drawing in the coyotes. How was I ever going to get him from where he was all the way to the house? And once I did, what to do with his body? I trudged back through the blowing snow to the house, and dragged a plastic sled I'd bought to haul hay bales up the hill to the mini mansion. Now I had to lift him and put him on the sled. Misty took time out from munching hay to come back up the hill to say goodbye, but Sunny didn't bother.

Churchill was in my way the whole time, trying to see what was wrong with his friend. Once I got Carbello situated, I grasped the rope on the front of the sled and pulled it behind me. Churchill led the way. It was slow going, and it didn't help that Churchie didn't want me to take Carbello, and he kept blocking my path on the only snowy, rutted track out of there.

By this point I was bawling both because of frustration with Churchill and from losing Carbello. Churchie would move forward a step or two, allowing me to drag the sled forward a few paces, and then he'd stop and block me with his body, and we'd be at a standstill, my face by his rear end. Finally I took my hands off the rope and physically shoved him forward to gain a few feet with the sled. Drag sled, shove llama, drag sled, shove llama. Churchill turned his head around to face me, his contempt and disdain for me utterly clear. His ears were pinned back, and he was definitely upset. But so was I. I had to get Carbello out of there, and I was freezing my butt off out there in my jammies, fighting with a stubborn, grieving, angry llama.

I may be strong, but loading a dead alpaca onto a sled, and having to repeatedly manhandle a 400-pound llama was too much for me. I snapped. We'd gone about twenty feet, and had reached an area of trees along the trail in the deep snow. I harkened back to how I'd dealt with BDL, the big damn llama I'd had to inject with dewormer. I body slammed Churchie into a small tree, wrapped my left arm around the base of his neck and the tree, and applied a full nelson. I grabbed his face with my other hand and pulled it right into mine. I yelled, "Listen, he's dead. He's fricking *dead*. Neither you nor I can do a damn thing about it so you had better get your butt out of my way *right now*."

Churchill looked at me and sobbed; tears spilled from his eyes in his grief about losing Carbello. I cried as hard as he did. I held onto his neck, put my face against him, and we cried together. But he still wouldn't move. I was so distraught I said through my tears, "Carbello, if you're still around here at all, you have to tell Churchie to let you go. He has to let me take your body out of here." Immediately, Churchill looked off behind my shoulder at something only he could see. I turned, but I didn't see anything. His ears cocked up as if he was listening to something, and then he turned and bent down to sniff at Carbello on the

Churchill the llama. To the left of his head is Carbello's wading pool, resting next to the tree I pinned Churchie against.

sled. He calmly turned and walked down the hill, and didn't block my way anymore. I'll never know if Carbello's spirit really was there, but something helped Churchill decide it was okay to let his friend go.

Misty and Sunny were down by the fence, eating hay. Some things take precedence, I guess. I stopped the sled to let them say good-bye to Carbello. They sniffed at his legs, and Sunny tried to chew on one of them. I had to pull the sled through the electric fence wires because the snow was too deep to open the gate. After some fancy and exhausting maneuvering, the sled was out, and somehow Carbello was still in it. I made my way across the yard, dragging the sled behind me. It was slow going because he weighed a lot, and it was hard to pull him in the sled along the deep, rutted trail in the thigh-high snow. Thankfully, I made it to the garage without him falling out, because I don't think I could have lifted him back into the sled another time. Completely exhausted, I left him in the garage, and I went inside the house, cried some more, and ate two brownies to take off the edge.

Since it was winter, and the snow on the ground was at biblical proportions, no measly Bobcat could dig a hole to bury him. I scratched my head trying to figure out how to dispose of his body. I called the town vet, who I've known for years, and asked him what I should do. He said he'd come to pick him up that weekend, and in the meantime, I should come to the vet clinic and pick up a Great Dane-sized body bag to hold Carbello. Once the vet picked him up, he'd put him in the clinic's freezer until they could send him off to be cremated, along with the other assorted animals who'd died or been euthanized. The vet is a bit of a rebel like me; he enjoys bending the rules, and getting away with stuff. When I wondered if the dog crematorium would take a dead alpaca, he told me, "No, no, get him in the bag, and they'll never know until they take him out to cremate him." We had a bit of a chuckle about it, morbid as it sounds.

My attempt to talk the vet into putting Carbello in the body bag himself failed; he was far too canny to fall for that. No, I had to do it. The fact it was winter was on my side, and the smell was far less than it could have been. After I picked up the body bag from the clinic, I drove home and opened the garage door. Yup, he was still there. Yup, he was still dead. Once I opened the bag, which was basically a heavy-duty plastic trash bag meant for dead bodies, I wondered, *Which end goes in first?* I held the bag out to measure the fit. Well, all of him would go in just fine, except for his long neck and head, which would stick out for all the world to see. And that would never do.

After some thought, I started with his back legs, and I won't lie, it was gross. He'd been dead a couple of days, and I don't know about you, but I'm not much for handling corpses. I picked up his two back feet, opened the bag, and slid it over them. Slowly I worked the rest of him into the bag, getting the whole torso in, but as I suspected, his whole neck and head were sticking out of the bag. That wouldn't do.

I had to figure out a way to get all of Carbello stuffed into the bag. The jig would be up if I used two bags—what Great Dane needs two body bags? Plus the long neck in one of the bags would be a dead giveaway this was no ordinary "dog." I did the only thing I could do: I bent his neck way, way back along his torso until his head was back by his butt. Once he was all stuffed into the bag, I tied it shut. I can't remember exactly, but I'm pretty sure I immediately went into the house and had a strong drink—right after I washed my hands, repeatedly. That was one of the grossest things I've ever had to do, and there have been plenty of them with all the stuff that happens around this place.

The vet is a busy guy, and it took a few more days before he could come out to get Carbello's body. The day before he arrived, I was out in the garage and heard rustling noises coming from the body bag. Envisioning a zombie alpaca apocalypse, I crept up on the bag, ready to run at the first sign of the raising of the furry dead. Rosebud was far braver than me, and went to investigate. A mouse darted out from inside the bag and ran off. He'd been having a bite to eat—a body bag buffet, if you will.

The vet showed up the next morning and backed his pickup up to the garage. We each took one end of the bag, and for some reason, I ended up with the heavy end, the one with the super-attenuated neck and head. Yech. It was gross all over again. We loaded the bag into the back of his truck, and he drove off to put Carbello's body in the clinic's freezer.

Wonder what they thought at the dog crematorium when they untied the body bag and realized, whatever the damn thing was, it sure wasn't a dog inside? I doubt too many people in the tony suburb where the crematorium is located have had much occasion to have seen or to know what an alpaca is.

A few months later I found a new home for Churchill. The mini horses were relieved—at least he wasn't going to be trying to suckle them any longer because he never did outgrow the behavior. A full-grown llama suckling a tiny mini horse? Definitely species-inappropriate behavior. The guy had some issues, obviously. Plus the minis never really liked him, so it was for the best. And Misty and Sunny moved into their garage stall soon after because it is much safer for them—the coyotes can't get at them anymore, although the annoying mice are still there.

Chapter 10

Rocky Raccoon

There's something about the front steps of my house—almost like it's a nexus for wildlife activity. Many of my encounters with the furry crowd have occurred there. I'm not sure why, but it certainly makes life interesting.

My illustrious airline job at one time forced me to start work at five in the morning. I don't know about you, but that is a really early start time, and it means you have to get up even earlier to get there on time. Now if I were one to primp, I'd need to get up at perhaps 3:00 or 3:30 a.m., in order to undertake full primping-ness. Since I was at that time employed in the cargo warehouse, the need for personal hygiene was somewhat reduced. The need for sleep trumped the need for beauty, and so I arose at the still obscene hour of four in the morning, totally groggy, with no time to make coffee. I had to let out the dogs, slog out to feed the horses and chickens, and take a quick shower to be out the door at 4:30 a.m. Then I'd race my car down the highway at ungodly speeds to make it on time to my incredibly fulfilling job.

This particular morning—I could argue it was still the night before, since it was pitch black outside—I hadn't fully opened the door before

Rosebud shot outside like a cannonball. She raced toward the birch tree about twenty feet away. I blinked the sleep out of my eyes, and had a momentary glimpse of three solidly built furry bodies with bushy, striped tails careening in all directions as my dog ran at them. Two of them made haste towards the woods, while the third bolted straight at me as I stood on the steps in my stupor, attempting to make sense of what was happening.

Rosebud, meanwhile, had realized she had completely misjudged the situation, and wasn't possibly able to take on three raccoons herself. She had gone to her happy spot under the bushes to hide, leaving me to take on a thirty-pound bundle of fur and snarling teeth, rocketing straight at me.

Yes, I had my trusty baseball bat. No, I didn't have time to raise it above my head in a display of clear dominance over nature. I did the next best thing—I snarled at Rocky the Raccoon like I was the biggest, baddest raccoon ever. I watched as, in midstride and only three feet from me, his eyes widened in alarm, and he attempted to skid to a stop, his claws scrabbling for purchase on the sidewalk. He executed a hasty turn and ran off down the front steps, only to hide under my car. I needed to be inside that same car—and driving off—in less than five minutes. No way was I going to try to get in the car with him right under the driver's door area.

His reaction to my raccoon snarl was so funny I didn't have time to be scared. The look on his face trumpeted, "Holy crap, that woman is nuts!" He stayed safely hidden under my car. I walked down there and I used my flashlight to see where he was. He looked back at me, blinking in fear. I used a really long stick to poke him in order to get him to move along, but he was frozen to the spot.

I went back in the house with the dogs, and decided I had time to make a cup of coffee. Forget being on time to work—I had a good excuse, not that anyone would believe me.

When I went back out fifteen minutes later and scanned the flashlight under the car, Rocky Raccoon had disappeared. I hopped in the car, fired it up, and rocketed off to work, burning rubber at every turn.

Chapter 11

Wing Swept

When I first got chickens, I was woefully unprepared. Similar to the question, "Which came first, the chicken or the egg?" my situation was more on the order of, "Which came first, the chicken or the coop?" The chickens did. And I had to scramble to come up with some type of housing for them, stat.

I settled on using the old dog run my dad built back in the 1960s. The floor was concrete, and it was enclosed on all sides with interwoven wire. Only problem was, the wire squares were too large, and a predator would have no problem squeezing in between and partaking of a fresh chicken dinner. I solved this dilemma by adding hardware cloth on top of the wire, and securing it with my usual standby, zip ties. Hey, it works. Looks terrible, but so what? When I got to the roof, I'd run out of hardware cloth, and instead put interwoven chicken wire across the top. I figured a predator would be stymied by the hardware cloth on the sides, and wouldn't bother climbing to the top and trying to get in that way.

My first chickens, Phyllis, Bette, and Sylvia moved into the refurbished run. They slept perched on a wooden dowel I had wedged crosswise halfway up the wall in one corner. They laid their eggs inside the old wooden doghouse, which had a small swinging door. Everything seemed to be going fine with this setup, although retrieving their eggs from inside the doghouse was a challenge.

Late one night, I was awakened by the loud sound of chickens squawking. This went on long enough I thought I should investigate. I stumbled my way to the dining room, turned on the backyard floodlight, and looked out the window to see what had gotten the girls into such a frenzy. Three raccoons, that's what, clambering about atop the run, searching for a way in. I opened the window and yelled at them. Six eyes reflected in the light, and thankfully they scattered. I went back to bed, pondering new ways to reinforce the chicken coop.

A few months passed, and all was well. The chickens were still among the living, and we had no new raccoon incursions. Then it happened again—I was jolted awake by panicked squawks. I didn't see raccoons clambering about their roof. This time it was two huge owls, flying like an aerial ballet, taking turns dive-bombing the girls where they perched. First one, then the other, swooped down in an arc at the chickens, hoping to somehow snag one in its talons. This time I had to go outside and yell at them before they would fly off. The next day, I hired someone to build a real chicken coop in the same spot—the Coop de Ville, the Fort Knox of coops. You'd have to use a bunker-busting bomb to get through the walls of that sucker.

No longer do I have to worry about the chickens being carried off by an owl at night, and I can enjoy the moments I catch sight of an owl winging silently off through the trees. You can usually figure out where they are: watch where the crows congregate, screeching at and mobbing the owl until it's had enough and flies away.

Several kinds of owls live around here. I've seen barn owls, barred owls, and great-horned owls perching on oak limbs in the woods at the edge of my yard during the day, and heard them hooting at night.

The Coop de Ville under construction.

Sometimes they are hooting right next to the house, in the birch trees—they must see my cats sleeping in the bay window, and hope to score a snack. It always makes me jump when I hear them so close; it's such an eerie sound.

One night I had fallen asleep on the couch, and decided I might as well stay there the whole night since it was just too much work to walk to the bedroom. Near dawn I heard a frenzied scrabbling in the rocks outside, followed by a high-pitched scream. I peeked out through the blinds and saw a great-horned owl on the sidewalk, wings outspread, a rabbit in his talons. I raced outside, probably to save the bunny—who knows, I was still half-asleep—and the owl flew off, leaving behind his kill. I checked to see if the rabbit was still alive, but it was a goner. I looked around for the owl, but couldn't spot him, and went inside to try and fall back asleep. Later when I went outside again, the owl had obviously returned, and flown off with the rabbit.

One morning I noticed my cat, Nutter, sitting in the window avidly watching something up above. A barred owl had snared his attention,

Nutter relaxing on top of an open door. His name suits him perfectly.

perched on a low-hanging branch of the tree within ten feet of the window. He and Nutter watched each other, and I was surprised neither one of them seemed to be wary of the other; it was more of a mutual interest.

A squirrel began making his way down the tree, heading right towards the owl. I nudged Nutter, "Hey, watch what's about to happen. *This* is why I don't let you go outside by yourself." The squirrel continued on down the tree until he got to the branch where the owl was sitting. He kept going until he was right behind the owl. The owl's head swiveled completely around, and it looked at the squirrel. The squirrel stopped in its tracks and returned the look, but he didn't seem scared. He didn't turn his furry little tail around and run away. No—they communed in silence for a time before the owl turned back around, and the squirrel scampered off with not a concern in the world, still in one piece.

That is *not* what I thought was going to happen, and I'm pretty sure my mouth was hanging wide open in surprise. Expecting that the owl would leap upon the squirrel and rend it asunder, I had been ready to cover my eyes because there'd be blood and guts and all manner of mayhem. But instead, it was two animals, one a predator, one prey, coming face-to-face and co-existing in peace.

Nutter lost interest and jumped down to the floor. The owl looked down at me, and we continued watching each other for a few minutes. He was so close I could see every detail of his feathers. I left him sitting on his perch in the tree, and went off to have breakfast.

Chapter 12

Coyote Code of Conduct

The coyotes around here seem to have no notion of how their species are supposed to behave. I guess it's because they're used to being around people. They trot through my yard at all hours of the day or night. They're equal-opportunity predators, and don't care what time it is because, for them, it's always chow time.

One day about noon I sat in my home office working on the computer. My dogs were hanging out on the front steps, while my mini horses were running loose in the front yard.

Something caught my eye, and I looked out the window. A coyote trotted by, five feet from the house, without a care in the world. I wouldn't have been surprised to hear the damn thing whistling a tune; it was so relaxed.

Well, that pissed me off.

It's bad enough it trotted past right outside my window, and my dogs and mini horses were in danger—but worse, the mangy bastard was lovin' life, with a big, slobbery smile on its deranged face.

I jumped up, opened the window and leaned out, yelling, "Hey! Get outta here!" The coyote stopped in its tracks and stood there, looking at me with mild confusion. It looked like a female; her coat a pretty rust color, but with a very skinny and rangy body. Her tongue lolling out between her massive pearly whites was rather off-putting, to say the least. She studied me for a bit longer before nonchalantly trotting off on her way to the woods.

I ran to the front door and got the dogs into the house before they scented the nearby coyote, because I could totally see where that would be going if they spotted her—downhill, fast.

Thank god the chickens were secure inside their coop. If they had been out in their chicken run, I would have been reclining in my hammock with a book, keeping a watchful eye on them while they pecked around in their not-so-secure enclosure, and Mrs. Coyote would have trotted right past me. I would have without a doubt fell out of the hammock in shock.

Didn't anyone tell that coyote she's supposed to hunt at night, not at noon? Isn't that supposed to be in the coyote code of conduct?

Chapter 13

Midnight Riders

Why does this stuff always seem to happen in the middle of the night? Another night, around 4 a.m., I was snuggled in my blankets, in a deep, sound sleep. Breezy slept next to me, hogging most of the bed like usual. One second I was blissfully asleep, bunched up like a pretzel, the next second I bolted upright in the bed, heart hammering. Breezy was howling and barking like a banshee. Something was outside.

Lurching out of bed and over to the window, I pulled back the curtain and, even without my glasses, I saw it: the reflection in the yard light of a number of eyes staring up at the house. They were too high off the ground to be coyotes. Could it be the bear that lives across the road in the regional park? Squinting harder, I realized they were horses. Four big honking horses were loitering in my front yard. Even for me, this was out of the ordinary.

Grabbing my glasses, I told Breezy, *"Shut up already, will you?"* and stumbled out to the living room, where I turned on the outside floodlight. Yup. They were still there. Nope. I wasn't hallucinating. I had to decide what to do about the four massive steeds in my front yard. Instead of doing the *normal* thing, the *rational* thing, I of course decided they needed me to help them. Help them how, wasn't part of the equation.

Dressing quickly, I went out the front door. The horses galloped off to my backyard. I hadn't had the foresight to turn on that particular floodlight, and the shadows were deep and black back there.

Hmmm. How to wrangle the horses? Oats! That's how. I went to the garage and scooped some oats up into my trusty ice cream bucket. I discovered this worked to get my mini horses to do what I want them to do. Bribery works every time. All I do is shake the ice cream bucket and say, "Crack, girls! Do you want some crack?" And they trot to me, licking their lips, as I dart into their pen, and they follow me in. Works like a charm. I figured it would work the same way with these behemoths.

Heading to the backyard with my ice cream bucket of tasty oats, I saw them under the black walnut tree. Holy mother of god, they were big. Did I *really* want to do this? Bring a bucket of oats out there with these midnight marauders? I was committed (I probably *should be*, committed, that is), and I walked slowly toward them, shaking the oats in the bucket. "Here, horsies…here, horsies."

Horses must have preternatural hearing because Misty and Sunny, at that time still living up in the pasture, heard me and whinnied, thinking I was feeding them. The four big horses' ears perked up, and they were off, thundering like a massive herd of buffalo through the backyard and up the hill in search of the whinnying minis. I started to think of them as the "Four Horses of the Apocalypse," because they were scary.

No way was I going to walk back there in the pitch dark, with those big guys running wild. Instead I made haste back into the security of the house to ponder my next move. The more I thought about it, the more I realized whose horses these probably were. The guy who had paid four million dollars for eighty acres of land up the road from me, and completely fenced it in solely for his four horses. Around here, that's a rather expensive "horse pasture." But rich as he is, I knew he wouldn't be in the phone book, although I had a general notion that he lived a few miles north of me in a new subdivision of McMansions. And I didn't know anyone else who would have his number.

So I did what I usually do in these situations: call the police and ask for their help. A very nice male officer showed up this time. I'm certain he already had been fully briefed on me, as he showed absolutely no expression as I described what had happened. I told him who I thought the horses probably belonged to, and he knew right away how to get hold of them. Remember how the woman officer who helped me try to get Sunny back inside the fence told me she had used her squad car to herd horses out on the highway? The horses out on the highway belonged to the rich guy. Thank heavens I'm not the only lunatic the police department has on their radar. It's heartening to know even rich guys can be a pain in the butt to the cops.

The officer said he would contact the horses' owners and have them come out to retrieve them. After he drove off, I went back inside and made a cup of strong coffee, since it didn't look like I'd be going back to bed any time soon.

A truck eventually pulled in my driveway and drove up to the house. The rich guy had a hired hand to take care of all his horses, in all of their many locations. By this point, the sky was beginning to lighten, but the sun had not yet risen. He and I walked back to the pasture and up the hill. There the four horses were, hanging their heads over the fence, talking to my mini horses, who were secure in their corral next to their mini mansion, a.k.a. a ramshackle three-sided shed.

We decided to put the big horses into the minis' fenced pasture because the minis would be safe from them inside their corral. The hired hand hadn't brought any halters, so I handed him the ice cream bucket for bait, and he led them down to the infamous gate, which

The big boys get acquainted with the mini girls.

now could be opened, thanks to my neighbor. All four horses went into the fenced in area and galloped right up to make better acquaintance with Misty and Sunny.

The hired hand then drove to Rich Guy's house to get halters and lead ropes. I retrieved my coffee and walked up to check on all of the horses. It was incredibly cute watching the horses interact because the big ones towered over the minis. The big horses couldn't figure out what the heck the minis were, and they were entranced as they leaned over the corral and sniffed at the girls. Sunny, meanwhile, was in love with the big boys, which made her kick, buck, and squeal loudly.

The hired man returned in his truck, along with the Rich Guy's wife—she looked as frazzled as I was, and she had worse bed-head to boot. They discussed how to get all four horses back to their pasture half a mile down the road. In the end, all he had to do was halter up the alpha horse, and the rest followed docilely behind. As he walked them through my yard past where I stood, their backs were at the height of my head, and I'm tall. They were huge. Rude damn horses; they shouldered me aside with disdain. Good thing I wasn't able to entice them with the oats, or I might have been a squashed lump in the lawn when they got through with me.

Off they went. The wife drove the truck while the hired hand marched off holding the halter of the lead horse, and the three other horses trailed behind in an orderly fashion. I watched them go up my driveway, and out of my life.

If anyone had been driving down the road at that early hour, it certainly made for an interesting and unusual sight. Let's hope no one witnessed the fact that the freak show parade emerged from *my* driveway.

Chapter 14

Raccoon Olympics

Breezy was already out the front door like a shot, Rosebud close behind, rocketing across the lawn towards their prey. I stumbled out the front door after them, laden down with a flashlight and my trusty baseball bat. It was pitch black outside, and I almost tripped over the bat as I rushed down the steps.

"Breezy! Dammit! Breezy, *get up here!*"

Yeah, right. As if she was going to listen to me when she had the bloodlust upon her. I peered out into the far edges of the yard where the dogs had disappeared, but couldn't see a thing. What I heard were growls, chirps, and trills. The dogs had treed a raccoon.

Aiming my flashlight in that direction, I scanned the trees. Yup. A pair of eyes shone back at me, reflected in the flashlight's beam. The raccoon looked to be about twenty feet up the old oak tree near the infamous coyote-chasing pond.

Breezy still wouldn't come to my calls and I heard her crashing about in the underbrush near the pond. Something else was crashing about right along with her. Rosebud, meanwhile, had retreated halfway up the lawn, and sat patiently waiting for Breezy to kill some varmints. Such fun!

I stalked across the yard, yelling for the dog to come, making sure my flashlight illuminated every nook and cranny of the woods in case something was deciding whether it should jump out at me. More crashing sounds ensued, and then the angry chitters and growls emanated from another tree. She had chased *another* raccoon up a tree. How many raccoons were out there, anyway?

My mind flashed back to the party of three raccoons several years prior that Rosebud had chased at 4 a.m., and how one of them had charged at me as I stood on the front steps. I didn't want to have to do my rabid raccoon impression again because I wasn't sure it would work twice.

Deciding it might be best to maintain a prudent distance from the activities, I stopped near Rosebud and waited. Periodically I scanned the light across the trees to make sure the eyes stayed where they were, and didn't make their way down the tree trunk. It was obvious from their continued vocalizations the raccoons were really upset.

"Breezy! Dammit!" From the splashing noises, I knew she had chased another one into the pond. Great. More splashing, more snarling, and more growling went on for a while, and suddenly Breezy ran out of the woods and past me up to the front door. Maybe she finally had enough, or maybe she had become acquainted with the raccoon's sharp incisors.

Whatever caused her to finally listen to me, she was ready to go into the safety of the house. I'm kidding myself here—the words "Breezy" and "listen" have no place in the same sentence. I trotted up to the front door and let her in, figuring Rosebud would be hot on my heels. Nope. She was still sitting in the yard, her head cocked in concentration as she listened to the splashing sounds. It sounded like something *big* was swimming with a strong, sure breaststroke, and was headed straight to shore with pinpoint accuracy towards Rosebud. I yelled for Rosie to come, but she was too caught up in the pleasant melody of large waves lapping on the shore—as the Creature from the Black Lagoon made its way ashore.

The creature gained hold on the muck at the edge of the pond. Cattails were thrust violently aside as it muscled through. I looked at Rosebud while I pointed my flashlight towards the woods. No eyes, not yet. The crashing and crunching of underbrush grew louder. It was definitely coming our way, and Rosie was a sitting duck out there in the middle of the lawn.

Dropping my flashlight, I clutched the baseball bat tighter, and hurried over to Rosie. I didn't have time to turn my eyes towards the woods, but I could tell the damn thing was nearly at the edge and moving fast, and I had a good idea it was a very angry raccoon. I grabbed Rosebud's collar and practically lifted her off her feet.

"MOVE, dammit!" This got her attention, and she turned tail and raced to the house. Now *I* was in the crosshairs, because she runs way faster than I do, but I still did my best impression of a fifty-yard sprint and made it to the front door. I flung it open, shoved Rosebud through, and jumped in after her. I'll never know how close that thing was on my heels because I didn't dare look behind me as I slammed shut the door.

Chapter 15

Misty Comes Calling

The first time one of the minis escaped was late at night. While watching TV in the living room, I kept getting distracted because of a weird noise coming from outside. It sounded like something was digging in the landscape rock next to the house. I peered out the blinds, expecting to see a raccoon lumbering past the side of the house.

Instead I saw a horse's face—Misty, the incredible escaping mini horse—looking in the window at me. I think she wanted to come inside with the rest of the herd (me, the dogs, and the cats). After all, it was the dead of winter, freezing cold, and pitch dark—prime coyote weather.

I'm afraid of the dark as it is, having read far too many monster books when I was a kid, and I think nearly every bump in the night is something coming to get me. Or else it's a coyote. Instead, I had to swallow my fear, suit up in my winter coat and moon boots, and go out to somehow capture my marauding mini.

I won't go into the pathetic details of how I chased her around the yard in the dark, and then tripped and fell face-first into the snow.

Perhaps Misty and Sunny have good reason for escaping...

Whee! She thought it was a big game, and I couldn't catch her. Finally I gave up and sat down on the ice-cold sidewalk next to my porch, and I'll admit it, I cried a few tears of frustration.

And the damn horse walked right up to me and nuzzled me, trying to make it all better. Ha! Fatal mistake! I leapt up, grabbed her, and held on for dear life while she tried to run. For such a little thing—about the height of a Great Dane—she is extremely strong. At last, I got her halter on, and led her back to the pasture.

Subsequent escape attempts involved Misty or Sunny individually, or sometimes together. I've lost track over the years of all their jailbreaks. I'm sure you're wondering why it was so easy for them to escape from the pasture. At the time, they were fenced in, and had the run of, several acres of pasture and woods and lived in their "mini mansion," the miniature horse version of a McMansion. A professional was paid good money to put up the electric fencing, and I forked out wads of cash to get the best electric fence chargers from Fleet Farm.

But sometimes even the best intentions go awry. Who knew electricity has a hard time making an uninterrupted circuit through three acres of fence line in a pasture covered in three feet of snow? My god,

Sunny plots her next escape on an icy winter day. The mini mansion is to the right.

I'm an English major—how would I ever know that? The minis figured it out; however, it took me a little longer. Too many times to count I took the shovel and dug out the lowest fence wires from the snowdrifts. I shudder to think of it now. Three. Acres. Of. Fence. To. Dig. Out. It was a complete nightmare, and yet I did it. Sometimes the solution was simply to recharge the car battery used to power the fence. I never figured out it was running low until the latest escape attempt. It's not like I was going to test the charge by putting my hand on the electric fence. Been there, done that. Ain't doing it again.

Yes, I did get smarter and bought some interlocking fence panels to attach to the mini mansion to make a large corral area. But I didn't go the next step, and put the mini horses in there at night because it would make too much sense.

On one of the many nights Sunny escaped, I was deep asleep, snuggled in my blankets. One of the dogs started to bark. Hearing what I thought was a subliminal whinny I decided I was hallucinating. You can see where this is going. I got out of bed, pulled back the window curtain, and looked out. Yup. Sunny, the incredible escaping mini horse was looking up at me. She then turned and galloped up the driveway. She trotted back to the house, and looked up at me. I glanced at the clock, and it was 4:30 a.m. on my day off work.

Winter. The dead of night. An escaped mini horse. That's pretty much the story of my life. I dressed in numerous layers of clothing, put on my boots, grabbed the flashlight and baseball bat, and went out the front door. Sunny allowed me to get the halter on her with relative ease (it might have had something to do with the bucket of oats I used to lure her), and I tied her up to the back of my Jeep while I tried to figure out what to do with her. If I took her back out to the pasture, she would escape again. I went in the house, made a cup of coffee, and considered my options.

At the time, the detached garage by the house where the mini horses currently live was filled with tractors and other implements, so I couldn't put her in there. However, the tuck-under garage beneath my bedroom was empty because I kept my Jeep outside. I led her into the garage and waited for daybreak, because I knew I'd have to dig out three feet of snow all around the perimeter to get the fence working again.

By eight that morning, I was fully caffeinated and ready to roll. I retrieved Sunny from the garage, and led her up to the sidewalk to go back to the pasture. I heard a whinny, and it wasn't Sunny. Here came Misty, galloping across the yard and onto the sidewalk. She came to see where her friend Sunny was. Now I had two escapees. Sigh.

It took me another three hours to deal with the fallout of the escapes. Shoveled three feet of snow along the fence—check. Wrestled the metal corral out of the thigh-high snow so I could open it to put the minis inside—check. And then the llama decided it was

It's only a matter of time before the next escape attempt.

a good time to start being amorous with me. Try trudging through deep snow with a fifty pound piece of fence section while a llama is intent on twining his long neck around your midsection.

In the interests of a sound night's sleep, that evening I lured all of them into the corral/mini mansion complex to feed them, and I locked them in there.

Chapter 16

Winner, Winner, Chicken Dinner

My chicken coop, a.k.a. "The Coop de Ville," is built like Fort Knox. The damn thing is so nice I almost moved into it myself when it was built. Nothing can get past the steel door or hardware-cloth encased windows. The outdoor chicken area, called a run, on the other hand, presents a far more permeable barrier to any varmint willing to give it a try.

Current wisdom on building a chicken run that's safe from predators instructs you to dig a trench angled outward completely around the area where you'll be placing the fencing. Once you've done all that digging, you're supposed to bury the chicken wire as a means to stop predators from getting under the fence and at the chickens. Hopefully the predator will give up and find something else to eat. That's the general idea, anyway.

However, since foxes and raccoons can easily chew through chicken wire, hardware cloth is a better choice. Kind of like window screen, it's made of hard, rigid wire, and is a bear to work with because it has to be cut with tin snips, and doesn't bend easily.

The hell with all of that, I decided, and pounded in some metal fence posts and zip-tied chicken wire to them. Next I bought some seven-

The Coop de Ville. It has since been painted barn red in a feeble attempt to make it look more like a chicken coop.

foot-tall bamboo poles, pushed them into the ground in a haphazard fashion inside the fenced-in area, and strung deer netting across the entire run. The bamboo poles served to hold the netting up high enough so I could still walk underneath. Lastly, I zip-tied the far ends of the netting to the fence. Half-assed? You bet. That's my middle name.

When I let the chickens out of the Coop de Ville, I make sure I'm nearby. My attempt at fencing does what it's supposed to—it keeps the chickens in, and the deer netting serves as a visual barrier to any hawks or eagles swooping overhead.

One day I was sitting on an upturned five-gallon bucket, hanging out with the chickens in their pen. I do this every so often because it's fun to watch them chase each other around when one finds a bug, and the others all want to steal it. In fact, they do this even when there's enough for everyone. They don't touch the food right in front of them; no, they want what *that* guy's got, and they won't be happy until they get it. They remind me of people that way.

Sitting on the bucket, I watched at least five chickens tearing around the run in wild pursuit of another one with something yummy in his beak. Suddenly one of the roosters looked up from pecking around, and actually paid attention to his surroundings. That's his job, and he had been totally sloughing off. He raised an alarm, and half the chickens immediately stopped whatever they were doing and hunkered down flat

The chickens pecking about in their run,
blissfully unaware of airborne dangers. Note
the haphazardly placed bamboo poles.

on the ground to make themselves less of a target, while the others peered around myopically to see what the fuss was all about.

There! The other chickens spotted what the rooster had seen. Feathered heads swiveled in unison, and tracked something in the sky. I must be dumber than a chicken because I was the last to look up and see what was incoming. And it was *big*.

Like a guided missile homing in on a target, here came a bald eagle. He had triangulated our position, and was locked in on our coordinates. He glided silently about fifteen feet off the ground, past the black walnut tree by the house. Less than thirty feet away, he was coming in hot.

Jumping up off the bucket, I stood in an attempt to draw his fire from the poor defenseless chickens, understandably quaking in their feathers. I yelled, "Hey! I'm in here too, buddy, so back off!" I plastered my most menacing expression on my face while all the while running through my mind was, *Omigod, look at that huge beak. Omigod, omigod. Look at those sharp talons!*

Obviously he realized I was a truly formidable opponent, simply on a cursory assessment. He broke off hostilities at the last moment, and soared past us out into the pasture. Turning to the chickens, I said, "Wow, *that* was a close one." My words fell on deaf ears, however; the chickens were chasing each other around again, completely ignoring me, their brave and valiant savior.

That was the closest I've come to a bald eagle, although I see them often, along with the hawks and turkey vultures, soaring high up above my house.

The encounter I had another day with a golden eagle was a bit more out of the ordinary. Driving back home down our gravel road, as I approached my driveway, something up above caught my eye. There's a cottonwood tree right on the edge of the road, and perched on one of the lowest branches was a huge golden eagle. I drove under him, looking up through my open window the whole time. He looked back down at me. The word *majestic* comes to mind.

A short distance up the driveway, I stopped the car, and kept watching him. Because I forgot to stop at the mailbox, I got out of the car and walked back down the driveway to get my mail. Not only didn't the eagle fly away, it continued to study me. I walked closer and stood in silence for at least five minutes as we looked at each other. I truly believe he would have let me walk right under him in the tree. It was an awe-inspiring encounter.

I'll never know for sure what type of winged culprit made off with one of my first chickens.

This was long before the advent of the Coop de Ville and other chicken security-related measures. While I ran errands, I had left Phyllis, Bette, and Sylvia running loose in the yard. Phyllis was a cool chicken, very friendly. Bette hated my guts, and wasn't shy about telling me about it. Sylvia, a consummate follower, could go either way. On the days she

Bette, Sylvia, and Phyllis free range in the yard.

was Phyllis' acolyte, she liked me, but on the days she was hanging with Bette, she despised me. I figured the three of them would be safe because I wasn't going to be gone long. Unfortunately, my short trip turned into several hours, allowing enough time for something to happen.

Upon returning, I looked around the yard to see where the girls were, but didn't see them. I called to them, making clucking noises. My neighbors don't have to pay for entertainment, they simply need to stand outside and wait for me to make animal noises.

Finally, here came Phyllis, her little chicken legs propelling her full-speed down the hill towards me. She was absolutely frantic, making panicked chicken noises, and it was obvious she was trying to tell me something had happened. Something bad. Unfortunately I flunked Chicken Speak 101. I picked her up and put her in the coop, and went out in search of Bette and Sylvia.

I walked the whole yard and called to them. Nothing. Next I went down to the front garden pond because they liked to hang out next to it. That's when I found the first clue: chicken feathers scattered about, some floating in the water of the garden pond—a *lot* of feathers, ar-

Bette and Sylvia check out the outdoor furniture.

rayed in a circular pattern. I looked up to the sky, and back down at the feathers. The way the feathers were situated, it looked like an impact pattern from above. Hawk, eagle, owl? I have no idea. There was no blood, so I thought there might still be a chance.

Calling their names, I walked back through the yard, and then sat on the grass in despair, feeling responsible for whatever happened. If I hadn't let them run loose, they'd still be alive. A chicken appeared, wobbling across the yard toward me. It looked like Sylvia, although it was hard to tell the three of them apart. She was really weak, and in rough shape. I brought her into the house, put her in a box in a spare room to rest, and went back out to look for the last chicken.

By this time it was dark and, although it was prime coyote time, there I was out in the woods with my flashlight, pushing through the sticker bushes and tripping over deadfall. For at least an hour, I pored over every inch of the woods encircling my house, trying to find the last chicken. No luck.

Before I went inside, I checked on Phyllis, all alone in her coop, and let her know I'd found Sylvia, because I thought she'd want to know, but that I couldn't find Bette. I went to check on Sylvia. She looked awful, with feathers missing, and she was hunched in her box with her eyes closed.

As an animal lover from way back, I'll do nearly anything to save an animal, if it's at all possible. So I did something most normal people wouldn't do—I brought her to the animal emergency hospital, which was the only thing open at that time of night.

The Twin Cities has four animal emergency hospitals, but only two would examine chickens, neither of them close to me. I drove Sylvia to the nearest one, which was all the way across the metropolitan area.

The same as any other emergency room, it took forever. The vet finally examined my chicken and took her off for x-rays. He came back after some time to say nothing was broken, but she had a number of deep puncture wounds. By this time, it was two in the morning, and I was exhausted. He kept her overnight for observation, and told me to come back the next night to retrieve her.

Heading home, I tried not to think about how much this was going to cost. I know, I know—if I were a "real" farmer, I would have simply gotten a shovel and whapped her over the head with it, and then used the shovel to bury her and been done with the whole matter. That's not who I am, not even close.

The next night when I went to pick her up, the vet said she wasn't any better; she was lethargic and wasn't eating. He brought her in to the examining room to let me see her. Her eyes blearily opened and she looked at me, and it was obvious she felt awful. He tried to talk me into putting her down, but after a bit of discussion, he decided to give her an injection of painkiller to see if it would help.

Why he didn't think of that when I brought her in the night before, I'm not sure. Once the painkiller kicked in, she was a brand-new chicken. Still not back to one hundred percent, but she was up and about, and interested in food. After this miraculous recovery, I brought her home, along with my much-lighter bank account.

Sylvia still wasn't strong enough to go back to the coop, so I put her in the bottom half of a kennel in the spare room, and she regained her strength in a few days. As she got stronger, her personality got stronger too—she bit my hand a few times when I put food in her dish. And she complained a lot in chicken talk. Sylvia would never do something that overt, so I attributed it to her ordeal.

Poor Phyllis was alone in the coop for days. Chickens are flock animals, but she did fine until Sylvia could rejoin her. A few days later, I went to check on them, and to reminisce about poor, lost Bette. I told Sylvia, "Yeah, Bette hated me. I know you were friends with her, but you know, she was kind of a little bitch, and hated me, but I still loved her. She was nasty to me, but oh well, now she's gone."

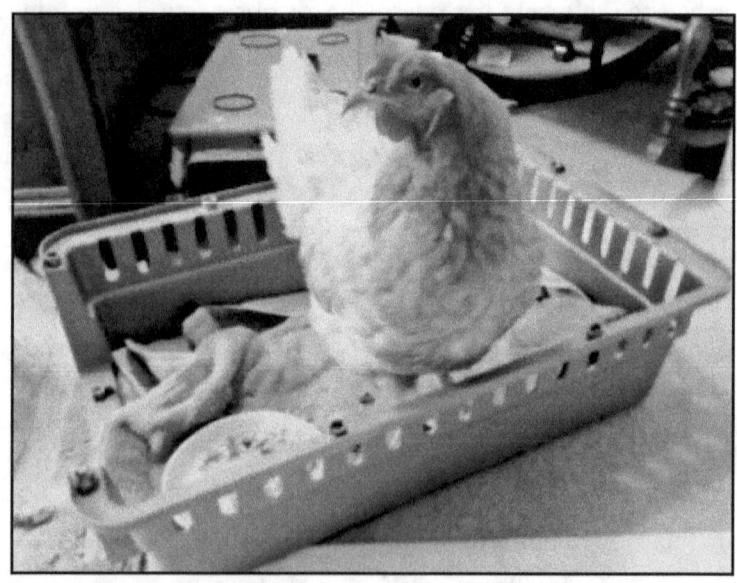

"Sylvia" shooting me an icy
glare while convalescing at home.

The whole time I eulogized the late, departed Bette the chicken, the more vocal and angry Sylvia became. It wasn't how Sylvia would normally act. I babbled on a bit more, as Sylvia stalked back and forth, chastising me. I stopped in mid-sentence and looked at her. I said, "Sylvia, you are acting so much like Bette, what has gotten into you?" She practically spit tacks at me with her reply. I'm pretty sure some choice chicken swear words were interspersed in there. That's when it hit me—the chicken angrily chewing me out wasn't Sylvia, *it was actually Bette*.

Once I finally had my light-bulb moment, Bette glared at me, turned on her heel, and stalked off, continuing to mutter to herself. As she hopped up onto her perch and disappeared into the nest box, I could swear her clucks translated to, "No shit, Sherlock. It's been me all along. You are *such* a dumbass."

Oops. And I called her a bitch to her face. Well, she was. She was damn proud of it, too, even after I spent a lot of hard-earned cash to save her feathered butt—without a single clucked thank you.

Chapter 17

The Great Mini Horse Escape

One hot summer day, I was doing laps across the yard on the lawn tractor, attempting to wrestle into submission the overgrown mess I jokingly call my lawn. All was at peace with the world—the dogs were napping on the steps, and the mini horses were out in their pasture, happily grazing.

At least I thought the mini horses were in their pasture. Wrong!

As I mowed my way towards the next swath of knee-high greenery, I glanced at the pasture. No minis in sight. I put the transmission into hyper drive, and cruised over to reconnoiter and assess the situation. In my life, "situation" is a word that brings to mind the old military term, "S.N.A.F.U." meaning, "Situation Normal, All Fucked Up." Yes, that is my life in a nutshell.

The minis were gone. They had somehow hightailed it out of the pasture, and in order to do so, they'd had to do the limbo underneath the electric fence wire. I wasn't sure how exactly those two extremely well-fed mares could have managed the contortions, but once again, they had. It's not like this had never happened before. The little vixens

Sunny and Misty's first day here. The overgrown, weedy lawn is on full and painful display.

had meandered down the trail to my brother's house, where the grass was greener and far tastier.

My brother and his family weren't home that day, and I'd somehow kept the mini horses' earlier escapes a secret from my brother. Although, since the minis had left several piles of "evidence" in his yard on their previous forays, I knew he was beginning to suspect.

It was too hot for me to contemplate walking all the way there to retrieve the girls. I hopped in my car, along with a halter, lead rope, and a bucket of oats, and drove down the road to my brother's house.

Immediately I spotted the minis near his propane tank, munching contentedly. They saw me drive up, get out of the car, and walk towards them. They darted to one side. I shook the bucket of oats, trying to earn their trust so I could lasso one of the little suckers and get a halter on her. No such luck—they were onto me. They danced away from me, and, after a hurried consultation with each other, broke into a spirited gallop, their long tails and manes flying, and they ran past me, down the driveway and to the road. Oh, crap.

Leaping back into my car, I put the pedal to the metal, gravel cascading into the air from my screeching tires as I sped off in chase. Two houses were nearby, and I pulled my car up on the road in front of them and got out. Where were the minis? The new neighbor, Bill, who I hadn't yet met, was out in his garden. I yelled up to him and asked if he'd seen my horses. He pointed over into the other neighbor's backyard, "You mean them?" Misty and Sunny were standing under the bird feeder, eating birdseed.

The two mini horses looked up at me for a microsecond, but quickly returned to their munching. The guy who lives there was doing yard work. He could see the mini horses eating his birdseed, yet he refused to help me catch them, and didn't even acknowledge my presence. Grrr.

Bill, the first neighbor, to his credit, did attempt to help me round them up. When I zigged, they zagged, making me realize how out of shape I truly am. The minis and I kept this up for awhile until they decided they'd had enough of me, and high-tailed it up another hill, underneath a fence, and disappeared from sight in the tall grass.

It was time to hang it up, go home, and nurse my wounds. With no idea where they'd gone, I didn't know what to do—and it was hotter than a convection oven. After sitting at home for a while, I became worried about them getting killed, so I hopped in the car to drive back down the road to their last known whereabouts.

Halfway up my long driveway my car, for no discernible reason, died and refused to start again. I got out, slammed the door, and cussed like a sailor. Now I had to walk a quarter mile down the road to the neighbor's house, with the ice cream bucket of oats in one hand, and the halter and lead rope in the other.

The horses were still missing, and I had no idea where they were. I was exhausted. I was pissed. I was sweating like a damn pig. I had had *enough*. I was fed up with the whole thing. I walked back to Bill's house, and since I hadn't had the chance earlier, shook his hand, introduced myself, and said, "I need a damn beer." It wasn't yet noon, but I didn't care. I took a huge swig from the beer can and said, "Nice to meet you."

I walked back up the road to my house, swilling beer the entire way.

When I did get back home, sweaty and completely done in, I decided to call the neighbors who live way up on the hill at the end of the road (yes, John, who always bails me out. Who else?), and ask if they had seen Misty and Sunny. They looked outside, and lo and behold, the minis were there, gallivanting with their huge stallion in his pasture. Somehow John and his wife, Diane, captured them and, after haltering them with the halters used for their mini-donkeys, led them back up the road, where I met them for the mini horse hand-off. I still remember the look Sunny gave me when she spotted me walking towards them, "Uh oh…the fun's over!" For me, the fun never started.

Chapter 18

The Turkey Trot

My dog Breezy thinks she's the biggest, baddest hunter around. First thing in the morning when I let her and Rosebud out the door to do their business, she's off like a shot, racing around the side of the house into the backyard, with Rosebud trotting along far behind. Excited barking ensues when she surprises a squirrel or two under the bird feeder, or gathering walnuts off the ground—and the chase is on.

Across the yard, back and forth, she and Rosebud chase the poor squirrels. Rosebud accidentally caught one once when she was younger. She was completely surprised, and she let it go—three times. It finally escaped to freedom up a tree. If the dogs ever did catch one, I'd intervene before matters went too far.

On another occasion, however, it wasn't squirrels that fled up into the safety of the trees. The usual excited barking began before Breezy had cleared the side of the house. But instead of the frenzied scrabbling sound of rodent claws in flight tearing into the bark of a tree, a new sound greeted my ears: loud flapping noises, and an angry screech.

I ran to the backyard to see what Breezy had gotten herself into this time. I arrived in time to see two huge birds take flight, and about twenty tiny chicks scatter in all directions, looking for a place to hide. Breezy and Rosie had no idea what to chase first. Breezy went for the excitement of flapping wings rising into the sky, while Rosie was too overwhelmed to do anything, and sat down with a huge smile.

The wild turkeys finally reached the oak trees, and alighted with an utter lack of gracefulness. They were very annoyed. They must have been on an early morning constitutional through my yard with their babies, which Breezy oh-so-rudely interrupted.

The babies were too small to fly, and they did the only thing they could—they found the closest hiding spot. I found one hunkered down in the woodpile; it was so cute. I tried to round up the dogs to allow the turkey moms to come back down and gather their babies in peace.

First I got Rosebud into the house, and almost had Breezy in, too, but she heard the enticing sound of giant wings flapping as the turkeys flew back to the ground. She wrestled free, and ran to investigate. I turned the corner of the house just in time to see something I never thought I'd see: Breezy, being chased across the yard by a very large, very angry mother turkey. I laughed to see Breezy's tail between her legs as she ran, looking fearfully behind her the whole way. The turkey ran full out after her, beak extended so if she caught her, she could peck Breezy to death. Who knew turkeys could run that fast?

After a few circuits around the backyard, Breezy made it to the door of the house, and scratched frantically to get in. Mama turkey broke off pursuit as I let Breezy in the house, and she and the other turkey mom rounded up all their babies and traipsed off into the woods.

The woods around here are full of wild turkeys. In the winter at dusk, if I look up the tall hill in the pasture, I can see big, black shapes roosting on the bare tree branches, and hear them "gobble-gobble" as they settle in for the night. The turkeys regularly come through my yard. Lately a group of three males come close to the back of my house most nights in their search for food.

A few days after I first saw those three, Breezy jumped onto the couch and barked like a maniac about something outside. Usually it's only a squirrel at the bird feeder, but this time it was a huge flock of turkeys. There were so many they flowed en masse up the hill on my front yard and into the backyard where they pecked around for acorns. I counted thirty-one turkeys. It was cool, although it's hard to fully appreciate the moment when a dog is barking full-throttle into your ear.

A few years ago, I looked out the front window to see a flock of at least twenty turkeys coming down the driveway towards my house. They paused on the lawn. I couldn't figure out what they were doing. It was like a convention, and one main speaker was doing all the talking—a large male turkey. He spread his tail feathers into a fan, and strutted manfully around in a circle as he spoke to his assembled admirers. Three other male turkeys fanned their tails, and retreated a few paces. Male turkeys have a long "beard" of feathers which hangs down their chest under their beaks, which is how I could tell them apart from the females.

The other turkeys milled around a bit, and a consensus must have been reached, because one turkey emerged from the crowd and timidly approached the leader. I still couldn't figure out what was going on, but it was fascinating. The lead turkey circled the newcomer, a female. He dipped his wings and bowed, and fanned his impressive tail a few times. He was courting her, and then he hopped on top of her and did the nasty, all while the others stood in a circle and watched.

For some reason it seemed like it was a really big deal to the turkeys, like it was some important ceremony. As I watched, I got that feeling—like maybe I wasn't supposed to be seeing it, like it was some secret ritual only the turkeys were allowed to see. Yes...I *do* have a vivid imagination, and always have.

When it was done, he hopped off, fanned his tail feathers a time or two, his three male companions fanned theirs, while his conquest dusted off her feathers and wobbled back to her girlfriends. He was the king, and she was his consort. It's all I can think of to describe it.

My own up-close-and-personal turkey encounter occurred one early morning when I drove to work. It was spring, and it was almost light at 5:30 a.m. I hopped in my little red sports car instead of the Jeep, since that's the kind of mood I was in that day, sporty—and rocketed down the dirt road after leaving my house. After driving a short distance, a large, feathered presence appeared on the edge of the road.

Stopping the car, I took a quick look. A big tom turkey strutted out onto the road and approached my car. He was a hottie; let me tell you. Tall, dark, and handsome—if you're a girl turkey, that is. When he passed in front of my car, I rolled down my window and looked at him. Turkeys mate in the spring, and this big boy was all fired up with testosterone, and lookin' for some love, and he was eyeing me with lust in his beady little eyes.

I'm ashamed to admit it, but I did laugh at him, just a little. I said, "You're not serious, are you?" He approached my open window with his tail feathers fanned out, like the drawings of Thanksgiving turkeys. He thrust out his chest to impress me with his manly physique, and made some come-hither noises deep in his throat. The damn turkey was courting me. Good god, he wanted to *do* me.

As fast as I could, I rolled up my window, telling him, "Hey, you're a really handsome guy, but you, umm, you really aren't my type…it's nothing personal, really...." I put the car in gear and burned rubber out of there, cackling to myself the whole way to work. I can't get a damn date, but at least the turkeys think I'm hot.

Chapter 19

Scrambled Eggs

On another normal, eventful day in my oh-so-calm and Zen-like existence, I ended up having to help a baby chick out of its shell. I was scared I was going to hurt it, not to mention outright kill it. It had tried forever to get out of the egg, and was getting weak. The hen was a first-time mother, and was completely clueless. I'd heard the peeping of a baby chick about to hatch the day before out in the coop, and periodically lifted up the hen to see if it had hatched. Its beak and part of its head had emerged, but the rest of it still hadn't made it out by the next day, which wasn't good. I rounded up the hen, put her and her clutch of eggs into a small dog carrier and brought them into the dining room, where I cordoned off and set up a hospital ward.

Rationally, I knew if a chick can't make it out of its shell by itself, there's probably a good reason, and it's best to let nature take its course. *Logically*, I knew I shouldn't bother. *Realistically*, I knew the odds were against success. The hell with that! *Rational, logical, and realistic* aren't in my vocabulary. Perhaps they should be.

Prior to commencing surgical procedures, I rooted around my house for the necessary tools, and found the perfect implement: a pottery needle tool, gathering dust in my art supplies. It's not like I'd had the time over the past few years to do any kind of art with all these animals keeling over dead left and right. Making time for creativity and fun? Ha!

At the hospital ward, I lifted the hen up from her eggs. There it was—its little beak and half its head crowning from the egg, but it was still breathing. One eye had emerged, and it was half-closed in exhaustion. In its frenzied attempts to break free from its prison, it had managed to make several hairline cracks in the rest of the shell, and that's where I focused my efforts. I held the egg, and carefully peeled little chunks of the shell off with the needle tool. Yes, I did sterilize the tool first—first in boiling water, and then in rubbing alcohol. I didn't use the good stuff—vodka—because I need to keep that in reserve for myself. God knows I need it, dealing with everything that happens around here.

The mom chicken watched me; I have no idea if she knew I was trying to help as I probed the egg further with the needle tool. She wasn't the brightest cluck in the coop. I never knew beforehand that inside an eggshell, there's a membrane around the chick, full of blood vessels—a chicken placenta. I tried to avoid the blood vessels, but of course a couple started bleeding a bit. I picked carefully at the shell and peeled more small bits away. The chick struggled, but was very weak.

When I got enough shell off, I pulled the placental membrane apart enough for the chick to get its wing out, which had to feel good for the little bugger. I peeled off some more shell, pulled some more membrane, until the chick finally struggled free of its shell, and popped out onto the surgical cloth, a.k.a., dishtowel. It had an umbilical cord attached to it. Never having assisted in a live birth, I'd never seen anything like it, and I just about puked.

I think I removed the placenta with the needle tool, but I don't really remember. I've blocked out the more gruesome bits. And no, I did not tie off the cord. I cupped the wet chick in my hands to warm it up and dry it. When it was strong enough, I held it up for its mom to look at: a bouncing baby ball of yellow-and-black fluff. I felt like the doctor in the delivery room. This was her first born, so it was a special moment. But the look in the mother's eyes wasn't adoration and love, no, it was full-blown panic. It was, *Ummm...Can we put it back? I don't think I'm ready to be a full-time mom.*

I laid the newborn on the towel under a heat lamp until it got stronger, and gave the mom a pep talk. I tried to instill confidence, and help her find some maternal feelings. She blinked at me in confusion. Well, okay, I'm not fluent in chicken-speak, but I thought she might get the gist of it. When I put the baby chick under her wing, the mom didn't know what to do. Then the baby popped out its tiny head and looked up at its mom, and she looked down at it, and it was true love. It was *so* cute. I wish I had a picture of the special moment.

After performing such delicate surgery, I was exhausted and took a well-deserved nap. When I got up, I heard *two* peeps coming from under her. Another chick had hatched, this one all on its own with no need for a midwife. I was now a proud chicken grandma, twice over.

Since I had to help the first chick figure out how to eat and drink, and it tottered around on unsteady feet, I named it Special Needs. It was a happy little thing, and spent most of its time snuggled under its mom's wing. The second chick had no problem figuring

Special Needs tucked under her mom's wing.

out how to be a chicken, and it looked healthier and stronger, and regularly knocked Special Needs on its butt.

The hen and chicks stayed in their digs in the dining room for a few more days until the chicks were strong enough to deal with the rough-and-tumble life out in the coop with the big chickens and roosters. I held out hope that the first chick would gain strength and live out a long chicken life. But sadly, it was not to be. I am saddened to report Special Needs passed on to chick heaven. She dodged death so many times in her short existence. I lifted up her mom periodically to check on the chicks, and found only the stronger one. I searched frantically and located Special Needs wedged in between the nest box and the wall. I have no idea how she made it all the way out there. Later the same day, I found her lodged underneath the baseboard heat register. On two separate occasions, I found her stuck to her mother's chest, close to death. But somehow, she revived each time and soldiered on.

On the morning of her passing, she had a few bites to eat and some water, and quickly snuggled back under her mom. When I went to check on her later, she was still tucked securely under the wing, but had already exited this earthly realm. I peeled her tiny corpse away from her mom, and set it down in the box to offer my condolences to her mother, who promptly got up and walked on her dead baby. Like I said, mama hen was a couple eggs short of a full carton; certainly not the brightest hen in the coop. Anyway, the other little chick is doing great. I call him Spunky, because that's what he is.

I'm not sure why I continue to let the hens brood on their eggs in the middle of winter, because the result is baby chicks born in the coldest time of the year. This necessitates me bringing the newborn balls of fluff into the house because the coop is far too cold for them to survive.

Last winter, two separate batches of eggs hatched out in the coop in January and, since the winter was a brutal one, the chicks had to come in the house. Their nursery was in the bottom half of an extra-large plastic dog kennel. A window screen covered the top, and a heat lamp provided warmth. First one chick hatched, and during the week, three more hatched.

When I brought the first chick into the house, he was weak, cold, and scared to death. I held him in my hands and tried to warm him. My fifteen-year-old cat Stripey was sitting nearby, and he came over to help. Maybe my life is different than other people's because I can let a chick run loose in the dining room, and neither my cats nor my dogs will hurt it. They leave them alone, even when the chicks come up and peck at them, or steal their food.

That day, after I set the chick down, Stripey sat down next to the chick and let it snuggle under his chest as he purred. He was mothering the chick, and helped to calm it down. It fell asleep under my cat, which sat patiently until the chick woke up. Then I put the chick under the heat lamp in the kennel. When the three other chicks were born, they all snuggled together in the kennel.

Before they got bigger and were feathered out enough to go back to the coop without freezing to death, I'd let them out to run around a bit on the linoleum

Stripey watching over the chicks

floor. It's easily cleaned up, so it's not like they were going to damage it. Stripey loved it when I'd put a chick on his back, and it walked up and down along his spine. It was like a free massage, and he absolutely loved when the chicks gave him a back rub. The chicks even gave Breezy a massage a few times. Rosebud, on the other hand, thought it was highly undignified for a dog to have a chick toddling around on its back.

When I've told my friends about some of the escapades with my animals over the years, they can't believe dogs and cats (and even the mini horses) could co-exist with chickens. I do admit to a bit of guilt, though, when I make chicken for dinner, even though I'd never eat my own chickens. It seems kind of hypocritical, and I always hope my chickens can't smell it on my breath.

Chapter 20

Muskrat Love

After I finished feeding and watering the minis in their pen in the detached garage, I decided to mosey out to the front garden pond to see if the water lilies were blooming. The dogs were nosing around in the front yard, safe for the moment, for once.

Halfway to the garden pond, movement off to the right caught my eye. *What the...?* At first I thought the small, brown, furry animal eating dandelions near the edge of the blacktop was a woodchuck. But when I saw the long, rat-like tail trailing behind a squat, muscular body, I knew it wasn't a woodchuck—it was a muskrat. Everything I know about muskrats told me, number one, it should be swimming in the water, and number two, why was it *not* swimming in the water, but instead walking around on dry land, eating dandelions?

The muskrat looked up and saw me, but kept munching with a total lack of concern. Something was off. Its behavior wasn't right. It wasn't the smartest thing to do, but I walked closer to it, to maybe fifteen feet away. It wasn't scared of me, which should have scared me. After watching it eat for a while, I noticed it was injured—something had taken a huge bite out of its back. I felt sorry for it, but what was I going to do—lure it into a pet carrier and take it to my vet? Sometimes I *do* know where to draw the line.

This was the first time I was so close to a muskrat. I had seen them swimming in the pond, their heads above water, a trail of waves spreading out behind as they arrowed through the water. And normally, once they catch sight of you, they immediately dive beneath the surface, and swim off as fast as they can.

This one's behavior was suspicious. It didn't seem like it was about to display violent tendencies, and rend the flesh from my body with its claws, but I decided it was best to leave it alone. I rounded up the dogs and headed back into the house, figuring it would wander off. The rest of the day, I kept the dogs close to me when they needed to go out to do their business.

Sure it would be gone the next morning, I was out feeding the chickens and horses, with the dogs running loose. Breezy started to bark near where I'd seen the muskrat the day before. I ran down there and saw Breezy ten feet away from the same muskrat. It was on its haunches, reared back, as it faced the dog. I'm not always the sharpest knife in the drawer when it comes to wild animals, but I was pretty sure the thing was rabid. A normal muskrat does not spend two days out of the water, on dry land, eating dandelions.

I remembered a symptom of rabies is a fear of water. Bingo. Everything fell into place. Breezy, for once in her life, listened to me and came when I called, and I hurried to put the two dogs in the house.

A few hours later I went back outside to see if it was still there. It wasn't. My feelings of relief were short-lived, however, because when I went out to my garden pond, the muskrat was eating in the flowerbed. Its back was still all torn up, but it didn't act like it was in any pain; in fact it looked practically tame. He looked up at me with his big brown eyes, with a stem hanging out of the side of his mouth as he chewed.

I have to admit it—he was really quite cute, in an overgrown rodent-like way.

Mr. Muskrat didn't make a move towards me. He was completely docile and calm, so I decided to leave him there, and check again later to see if he was gone. The dogs and I made a run in the car to Dairy Queen for a hot-fudge sundae and two pup cups. As I drove back down the driveway, I stopped where I'd last seen the muskrat, and leaned out to look. There he was, in the same place, but now he was curled up in a fetal position, looking very dead.

After I parked the car up by the house and got the dogs safely into the house, I went down to check on him. If he were dead, I'd need to somehow remove him so my dogs didn't chew on him. The dogs were current on their rabies shots, but I didn't want to take any chances. I grabbed a shovel to pick him up, although I wasn't sure what I was going to do with him afterwards. But wouldn't you know it, once I got to where his cold, dead corpse was supposed to be, he was up and about, eating again.

That clinched it for me—he was definitely rabid, and I was definitely freaked because I had to get him out of there. I couldn't spend days worrying about my dogs tussling with him, or possibly being attacked myself. I drove down the road in search of a neighbor who could help me figure out what to do. I knew I wasn't up to cold-bloodedly braining it with my baseball bat. Maybe one of the neighbors had a shotgun, and could put the poor thing out of its misery.

I was in luck. Several guys were standing out in the road in front of one of the houses, along with a neighbor on a four-wheeler. Pulling up, I rolled down the window, and without any preamble, said, "Does anyone have a shotgun?"

Probably not your typical opening, since I recognized only one of them, but I didn't much care. I was nearing my breaking point in dealing with the ongoing wild animal extravaganza on my own. Once I explained the situation, the neighbor on the four-wheeler fired it up and followed me back to my house. I showed him the muskrat, which had now resumed the fetal position, looking once again like it had gone to the great beyond.

We didn't have a shotgun, but we had my baseball bat. No, the neighbor didn't use it to brain the poor creature—but to poke at it to see if it was alive. Yes, definite signs of life as it uncurled and sat up to blearily look around. We both backed off a couple of paces. He must have been an animal lover, too, because he told me to get something to put it in, and he would "take care of it."

Not wanting to go into the specifics of what exactly "taking care of it" might mean, I rushed to find something he could use. Since I'm not equipped for wild animal removal, I came up with a paper grocery bag and a large plastic trash bag. I handed both to him before retreating several feet. He kept the bat in his hands to prod the muskrat into the bag, but once he put the open grocery bag on the ground in front of it, the muskrat walked right into it and lay down. It was truly bizarre.

The guy picked up the bag, popped it into the plastic trash bag, tied it shut, and put it on the back of his four-wheeler. And off he went, to "take care of it."

A few weeks later I saw him by chance. In my life, "by chance" means something has once again hit the proverbial fan, and in this case, life ran true to course. I was driving down the road on my way to work, late like usual. I'd driven maybe half a mile when over a small rise came two thundering horses, lathered and wild-eyed, galloping straight down the center of the gravel road. I slammed on my brakes to avoid a head-on collision, and jumped out of my car to try to stop them.

Don't ask me what I was thinking—because I wasn't. I was in full I-have-to-rescue-the-poor-things mode, like usual. These big honking horses were fully saddled, haltered, with their reins flying loose in the air. But they had no riders. One horse tripped when a rein went under its front hooves, and it almost went down in front of me. They were crazed with terror, and I was going to try to catch them. Good Lord, when will I ever learn?

My mini horses come when I call to them with my version of a whinny, and so I stood in the middle of the road, in broad daylight, and whinnied at the top of my lungs. It's a damn good thing I can't see what I look like when I do stuff like that, or I'd have to go into hiding for the rest of my life. But the horses heard, and responded. They put on the brakes, skidded about ten feet, and did a complete U-turn. Now they were galloping right back at me.

Waving my arms, I made calming horse-type noises. They thundered past in full-blown panic, just feet away from where I stood. Suddenly they turned and galloped up a long driveway. I watched as they reached the house and blasted past it to points unknown. A woman appeared up by the house and looked down the driveway at me, and from several hundred feet away I could interpret her expression as, *"What the?!"*

My car was sitting in the middle of the road, motor running, with the driver's door wide open. I ran up the driveway, and when I got up to the house, along with the owners of the house, there was the neighbor who helped me with the muskrat. He looked at me as he sipped his beer, and said something to the effect of, "Shit just seems to follow you around, doesn't it?"

Once I explained what was going on with the horses, which by now had raced off into the back forty, I told them I thought maybe the owner might be the Rich Guy, he of the Four Horses of the Apocalypse that showed up in my yard in the middle of the night. These neighbors had the phone number of the Rich Guy's hired hand, and they called him to come rustle up the horses.

By now I was running even later for work, and said my good-byes. Before I turned to walk back down to my car, I asked four-wheeler guy what he did with the muskrat. "Oh, I didn't kill it. I drove it down the road a ways to another pond, and let it go." Since there aren't too many houses on our road, and it's still fairly rural, it was probably fine, especially since Mr. Muskrat didn't look like he had much longer before he made his final trek to Muskrat Heaven.

And the crazed, marauding horses? They weren't Rich Guys. It turned out the horses had spooked on a trail in the regional park, thrown their riders, and galloped off. The hired hand, who unlike me must be a horse whisperer, easily caught them, walked them up the road to the trailhead of the horse park, and reunited them with their owners, who were frantically looking for them. All ended well…this time.

Chapter 21

The Bobcat Saga

On a balmy evening in late May, I got home from work at seven, and let the dogs out to sniff around and do their business. Next I liberated the mini horses from their stall, and let them scamper about loose in the yard for a tantalizing dinner of Creeping Charlie, assorted dandelions, and sundry other weeds. If they could find any grass in the jungle of overgrown green weediness I call a yard, I'd be surprised. When I'm not home, the horses spend their days in the detached garage in a large pen where they are safe from the loitering coyotes.

Once all the animals were doing their thing, I sat down on the front steps to read before it got too dark. My relaxation was immediately interrupted by the dogs barking at something in the woods at the edge of the yard. I put down my book with a muttered curse or two, and walked all the way down there to see what in god's name had them so excited. Once there, Some-Damn-Thing snarled at me. My first thought was, *Holy crap, what was that?* My second thought was more of the same.

Xena Warrior Princess that I am, I yelled at Whatever-It-Was, and it ran. Fast, all the way around the edge of the yard in the woods, to the backyard—hundreds of feet in mere seconds. That thing moved like a bat out of hell. And for some reason I wasn't scared. Yet.

The saga of the Snarling Beast From Hell continued the next day when I went out to the horse pasture (where the mini horses used to live, B.C.—before coyotes) around noon to look for morel mushrooms. The dogs were lounging a couple hundred feet away in the backyard. Of course, since the mini horses were in their stall in the garage, I was completely, utterly, stinking alone out there. I was armed and dangerous—me and my empty ice cream bucket.

Soon I found a monster morel, and another smaller one. I walked a little farther back in the pasture. *SNARL*. The exact same kind of snarl as the previous night. I looked up and into the underbrush edging the fence, but couldn't see anything. *SNARRRLLLL,* this time with a tad more emphasis. I looked again, with a bit more concern. There it was again: *SNNAAARRRLLL,* as in, "Hey, idiot. Yeah, you. I'm talking to *you!*" I bent over and picked up a sharp stick with which to defend myself (yeah, right. like that's gonna do any good), and said, "Okay...okay...I'm leaving," to whatever was watching me.

Wasting no time getting out of there, I walked as fast as I could, looking back over my shoulder the whole way. One of the dogs was going crazy back in the yard, barking like a maniac. I almost fell on my face trying to get through the fence wires to get out of there. Good thing the electric fence wasn't running, although I probably would have still gone right through it.

I strong-armed both of my dogs, and we all retreated into the fortress-like interior of the house. I'm not ashamed to say I immediately locked all the doors, too.

Once I got my pulse somewhat below coronary level, I called my friend Bridget and related my story, and how I thought it was probably a bobcat. I remembered my mother told me she saw one here about twelve years before, when it crossed the frozen pond in the middle of winter.

The guy Bridget works with (I call him Rambo—he's a hard-core hunter I let hunt deer on my land) scoffed and said it was probably a raccoon. I told her to tell Rambo I have been snarled at by raccoons—and *that was no damn raccoon.*

The encounter out in the pasture really shook me up, but I had to get ready to go to work at the illustrious car dealership where I was now working. Rather than actually doing work once I got there, I instead went online and looked up everything there was to know about bobcats. I learned among other things, yes, they do indeed eat mini horses. More enlightening: they can successfully whack a human if they feel threatened.

These immeasurably helpful articles described in great detail how a bobcat would go about doing in a human: they go right for the neck and rip out the jugular. Good lord. I must have read that particular passage out loud in stark horror, because a customer standing at the counter told me, "Oh, it was probably a cougar. My parents have them in Afton."

The situation keeps getting better and better, doesn't it?

Bridget had listened patiently when I called and described, in painstaking detail, my encounter with the skulking creature in my woods. However, I was shocked when she told me she'd still be waiting for me at my house that night when I got home from work so we could look in the pasture for morels. I told her she was nuts.

But when I drove down my driveway, there she was, sitting in her car, waiting. Resigned to my fate, I simply looked at her, went inside the house, got a big glass of wine and my baseball bat, and followed her out to the pasture to look for morels.

Bridget was totally calm out in the horse pasture as we wandered about, poking around in the grass for morels. She didn't blink when something went crashing through the woods where Whatever-It-Was had been earlier in the day. She looked for morels as I monitored the perimeter, drank my wine, and brandished the bat.

We managed to make it out of the pasture, and then we went down the wooded hill to the pond (the one where Breezy delights in chasing coyotes), searching for the elusive morel. We made it safely back up into my yard, where she said, "Oh, what's that?" A baby raccoon, that's what, lying there, all alone in the grass. Don't ask me where mama raccoon was because I sure didn't want to know.

We walked all the way up the driveway and into more woods. We heard a sudden flurry of noise, and something darted out of the brush at us. I lifted my bat in a defensive maneuver to fight off whatever brutish beast was about to attack us, but it was only three little bunnies. They stopped two feet away and stared at me. Like I said before—*Good lord.*

We walked on, still on the hunt for morels, and wouldn't you know it, a wild turkey flew up from the underbrush, landed in an oak tree, and looked down at us from his perch. The bunnies came back out and ran past us. If I were one to do drugs, I'd think I was on some kind of acid trip because it was that bizarre.

We walked back down the driveway. The baby raccoon was still there. It probably still is. I don't care. I made it into the house in one piece. Thank god. Unfortunately the wine was all gone, and we hadn't found one damn mushroom.

Chapter 22

Roadkill Cafe

On a gorgeous summer day, I took Breezy and Rosebud on a two-mile walk down our gravel road. We meandered along, the dogs snuffling happily, darting to and fro on their leashes as they caught scent of some new delicious aroma.

We continued on in this way, with me periodically being jerked nearly off my feet by one dog straining at her leash toward one side of the road, to the other dog hauling me to the opposite side. In between having my arms and shoulders nearly separated from my upper torso, I had to continuously unsnarl their two leashes.

In the midst of this mayhem, I somehow noticed a turkey vulture sitting high up in the limbs of a dead tree, not forty feet away. It was watching as we ambled by, probably amused by our stumbling progress. The dogs and I walked nearly a mile to the end of the road before turning back. They could have gone on forever. I, on the other hand, was almost done in, although for once I wasn't gasping for breath like a dying fish. Seriously-out-of-shape is my middle name.

When we neared the area where I'd seen the vulture, I saw he and his girlfriend were now standing on the edge of the dirt road dining with relish on a freshly killed rabbit. At least I think it was a rabbit. What I could see looked like long strands of spaghetti being pulled up, and then quickly gobbled down. It looked kind of cool until I realized they were chowing down on the intestines. Their big bald heads dipped down, and pulled up a big spaghetti noodle of an entrail. It wasn't as gross as it sounds, and it was obvious they were enjoying each succulent bite.

Fascinated, I watched them as the dogs and I walked closer. The vultures were fully aware of our presence, but they let us approach to within thirty feet. I was surprised my dogs hadn't already started to bark, but they, too, were fascinated. When someone drove past in a car, the female vulture took off in flight, up over the pond, while the other vulture continued with his lunch. She flew in a long, looping arc over the water, and then circled back, swooped down, and flew low over our heads. A strafing run—and yes, I ducked, wouldn't you?

Breezy couldn't take any more, and started barking. The female vulture winged her way off, heading for points unknown, but the male stayed and kept eating with complete nonchalance.

He let us walk right by him as he dined. I had to hold the dogs close as they strained at their leashes, but we all made it past unscathed. It was incredibly cool. Vultures are huge birds, fully as big as the bald eagles I also see around. For all of their supposed ugliness, vultures are incredibly graceful in flight, and I love to watch them soaring like eagles on the updrafts on their out-swept wings.

Seeing the vultures that day put me in mind of another encounter I had with them another summer day a few years before. It was hotter than bejeezus, and humid, to boot. The typical Minnesota summer day with 98 degrees and 80 percent humidity: stand in one place, and you're nearly drowning in a pool of your own sweat. And you'd have to be completely nuts to engage in any form of exercise.

Ah yes, the perfect day to install my new garden pond.

I had hired a guy with a skid loader to dig a shallow area for my pond. I let it sit for months, too lazy to get around to doing the rest of the work—until the hottest, most humid day of the summer thus far. Yes, that was the day I finally got off my butt and decided to finish the pond. Over the years I've put in three garden ponds. Each of those times I did it on the most ungodly hot and uncomfortable day possible. I'm not sure why that is, but I wish I wouldn't do stuff like that.

I dragged the rubber liner that weighed at least a ton out to the hole patiently waiting in the dirt, and traipsed back to get the underlayment. When I tore out the carpet in the house, I'd saved the old padding and now I dragged out all the varied and sundry pieces. I dug around in my garage, trying to find a shovel to even out the dirt on the edges of the pond, and to backfill, where needed. This endeavor took the most time because I wasn't the most organized person back then.

Once I had all the correct implements and materials, I set about constructing the pond. Unrolling the padding, I tucked it on all sides and on the bottom of the dirt hole. I manhandled the black rubber liner—boy, that sucker had gotten really hot in the sun—and unrolled it across the hole. It took forever to get it just right, with all the edges equal until the entire hole was completely covered. I probably could have filled the pond with all the sweat pouring off my body, thanks to the heat.

Staggering back to the house, I dragged the myriad loops of garden hose all the way back to the quasi-pond, untangling them and periodically tripping over the coils. After I placed the hose nozzle in the center of the new pond, I staggered all the way back to the house to turn on the water. Right about then, I was wondering: why didn't I put the damn pond closer?

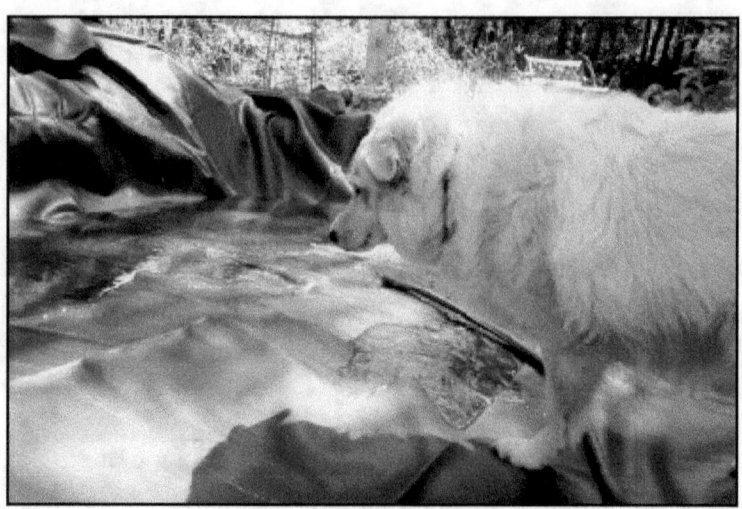

Rosebud supervising the filling of the new pond

Success! The pond was filling nicely. The dogs wandered back to investigate and immediately waded into the rising waters. I had a real pond.

I collapsed on my back on the grass near the pond, panting from my strenuous exertions. After several minutes I got the creepy feeling I was being watched. I slowly opened one eye and looked around. Nothing was in the yard, the dogs had wandered back to the house, and I was alone.

Glancing skyward, not more than fifty feet directly above me, a vulture was doing lazy circles, looking down at me. I watched, stupefied, until I suddenly realized what a circling vulture means. Ignoring how completely exhausted I was, I jumped to my feet and bolted for the house. Did he think I was roadkill, and it was his lucky day—he could eat for a week? What would it have been like if he *had* circled down and alighted for a closer look—and I had opened my eyes to see a vulture standing next to me, eyeing my carcass for the most succulent bits. This time the neighbors might actually have called the cops, because the screams would have been bloodcurdling.

Chapter 23

A Rabid Coyote

Going up against a coyote that has all its faculties intact is one thing. But doing so with a rabid one, in my thinking, is the stuff of nightmares.

My first inkling of what a rabid coyote was capable of came in early September when I was in northern Minnesota for my niece Callie's wedding. The next morning my friend Anita and I were on our way to breakfast, chatting as she drove. Suddenly the truck in front of us slammed on its brakes, and began to veer wildly across both lanes. "What the heck?" we both said. And then we saw it—a large, crazed-looking coyote, leaping up repeatedly at the truck's passenger window. It ran off toward the ditch, but charged back at the truck, again and again. It was attacking a damn *truck*. It was beyond scary to see, and we both came to the same conclusion—it was obviously rabid. At last, it darted off into the woods.. As we continued on our way, I regaled Anita with my own coyote stories.

Fast forward a few months to the dead of winter, at around ten in the morning. My dogs, Breezy and Rosebud, had been outside on the steps, hanging out, communing with nature. Both dogs got cold, and

Breezy came inside and sacked out on the couch. Rosebud decided she wanted to go sit in the back seat of the car to stay warm, so I left the car door open while she napped. The mini horses were ensconced in their pen in the detached garage close to the house, happily munching on hay. Their big garage door and the service door were both open.

I puttered around in the house, cleaning or something. Okay, cleaning is a stretch. I was probably reading a book. When Breezy barked like crazy at something outside the living room window, I decided I might as well see what it was. Another squirrel, or perhaps a bird or two? Ha! It was a coyote, tottering along on the lone path in the knee-high snow which I had trail-blazed up to the chicken coop. Tottering is too generous a word for what it looked like as it lurched zombie-like towards the house. The coyote was mangy, and looked weak and seriously disoriented.

The coyote rested for a few moments, while Breezy continued barking and leaping at the window. It resumed its wobbling journey towards the house, one unsteady step at a time. I mentally wiped my brow and thought, *Whew! Am I glad all the dogs are safe inside because that thing looks like it's rabid...*and I realized, *Oh, no!* Rosie was still outside, and right in the line of fire because, when the coyote ultimately made it off the snowy path to the sidewalk and steps, it would totter right past the open car door with Rosie snuggled inside. And right after that, it would meander past the minis in the garage.

To say I completely freaked out is an understatement. I ran to the front door, with Breezy hot on my heels. I put on my boots and winter coat, grabbed the baseball bat just in case, put my hand on the doorknob and thought, *Am I actually going to go out there and do this?* Yes, I was.

I manhandled Breezy away from the door, telling her, "You *really* don't want to go out there, Breezy," all the while thinking, *Then why am I?* I cautiously opened the door and poked my head out, and looked towards the corner of the house where the coyote was headed the last time I saw him. The coast was clear. Before I could consider the concept of "Actions vs. Consequences," I was out the door and running as fast as I could down the steps to the car. "Rosie! Stay! Coyote!" Next I ran to the big garage door. The mini horses looked up at me while they chomped on their hay, I yelled "Rabid coyote!" in explanation. I slammed the big door closed, and ran back to the service door, while I kept an eye out for the coyote. The coast was still clear. I slammed shut the door and dashed to the car. I grabbed Rosie, shut the car door, and we both ran to the house.

We made it up the steps and almost to the front door when, like the Great White Shark in *Jaws*, the coyote surfaced. It poked its head around the corner of the house and peered at us, its tongue hanging crookedly from its mouth. Rosie and I stood on the steps staring at the damn thing only fifteen feet from us, so close I could see clearly see its fangs. I couldn't help it—I screamed. All the other times I've faced down coyotes, I wasn't terrified. Scared, yes. Angry, yes. Terrified? Not until I faced a rabid one.

My screaming didn't have any effect on him. I waved my arms; I waved the baseball bat. For once I didn't pull the whole Xena Warrior Princess schtick and run straight at him. Perhaps I am not, after all, certifiable. Instead I yanked open the house door, shoved the dog through it, and darted in after her.

Holy crap. After I slammed the door and locked it, I collapsed against it for a minute before I was capable of making it back up the stairs into the living room. Yes, Breezy was still barking like a fool. I walked over to the living room window with nearly as unsteady a gait as the coyote's, and watched as he wobbled his way past the front of the house and down to the driveway, where he continued at a glacial pace to points unknown.

In a way, I felt sorry for him because he was totally out of it, but I also didn't like that, in broad daylight, he was directly outside my living room window. A furry peeping Tom, if you will. My hands were shaking so much if there were a Richter scale for shaking hands mine would have rated a 10.0. I didn't care it was only ten in the morning because this situation called for stiff measures—or a stiff drink, which was my choice.

And the kicker was I was more scared for my dogs and horses than I was for me. And for once I couldn't imagine myself fighting off the thing, though it was far smaller than the ones the dogs and I faced down earlier. All I could think about was the close-up view of its fangs—and me having to get rabies shots.

As I glugged down my incredibly strong vodka concoction, I reflected on the other times I've interacted with crazed varmints at this house. I've been charged by both rabid skunks and a rabid woodchuck, which just kept coming. The rabid woodchuck came at me years ago as I tried to walk down those same front steps on my way to my first day at my illustrious airline job. Perhaps it was attempting to warn me away from making one of the bigger mistakes of my life, but instead I yelled for my brother, who came outside with a shotgun. It took five blasts at pointblank range before it gave up the ghost. I blithely continued on to my new job. Now I know I should have paid attention to the woodchuck's omen.

I don't know if the rabid coyote had such a message for me. Perhaps it was to realize my courage does have limits, and maybe that isn't such a bad thing.

Chapter 24

Sting Like A Bee

My day-to-day routine of fending off the local predators in ferocious hand-to-snout combat doesn't always involve coyotes, bobcats, or the local bear. Sometimes the fight to the death involves something far more nefarious and terror-inducing—winged predators like wasps, hornets, and bees.

How many times have I been stung? Too damn many. And yet when I see a wasp in the house, I invariably scoop it into a plastic container, and take it outside to freedom. I continue to do this even after all the times its evil compatriots have stung me. Obviously, my mercy knows no bounds. Either that, or I'm a flaming idiot.

One fine day I set out into the far reaches of my yard, equipped with a shovel and a wheelbarrow to dig up and move some perennials. All was going stupendously well, although my energy level was flagging a bit, exercise being against my better nature. I had just dipped the shovel deep into another bit of dirt and bent to lift up the peony I was moving when I heard a deep, reverberating hum coming from the ground beneath the peony. Thank god for the human body's innate sense of self-preservation, because that ominous sound had me sprinting from zero to fifty in less than a second.

When I got to where my body, in its infinite wisdom, had finally stopped, my brain attempted to catch up with the proceedings. Looking back at where I had dropped my shovel, I watched as a huge black cloud arose from the earth. It swirled and moved menacingly in search of whatever had caused the disturbance—which was me. I could hear the angry buzzing from where I stood.

It's a good thing those little bastards don't seem to have very good long-distance vision, because the object of their rage was standing right over *there*, and all they had to do was move their horrendous black cloud of angry, roiling ground hornets twenty feet, and they would have been upon me. And it would have been the end of me. As it was, one bright and enterprising individual peeled off from the milling mass, arrowed straight towards me—and nailed me. I smashed him into a black and yellow smear to reward him for his efforts as I ran toward the safety of my house.

I made it out of that particular encounter relatively intact. Future encounters, however, took a different course. One day I walked out of the pole barn and noticed a large paper wasp nest tucked up in the corner of the open roll-up doorframe. The nest was a big one, and I could see the wasps flying to and fro in their endeavors. Standing back a pace to make myself seem less a threat, I admired its construction. What can I say? It was a really cool-looking big wasp nest. A wasp hung motionless on the outside of the nest, watching me. Our eyes locked. Big mistake, because I could see in his multi-faceted waspy eyes that he had decided I needed to be taken out, posthaste.

That S.O.B. had me in his sights, and he powered up and took wing, like a fighter jet locked onto its target. I had no time to run, and nowhere to hide. I had managed to turn sideways in my feeble attempt at escape when he got me, right on the back of the neck, near my brain stem. Attila the Wasp continued drilling into my flesh while I attempted to dislodge him from my neck as I ran down the hill. Perhaps he had run out of ammunition because he eventually disengaged his stinger, and I was free.

As I pounded in terror down the hill towards the house, my thoughts were in a frenzy. *Oh my god, he got me in the spine. He knew exactly what he was doing…he was trying to KILL me! Shit! The venom will travel directly to my brain, and I'll be paralyzed. Run! Faster! Shit. Shit. SHIT!*

Tearing open the back porch door, I ran through the kitchen to the cupboard holding the Benadryl. Lounging cats dove off the couch in all directions, and took cover. Vitamin bottles and various other things were tossed en masse onto the floor as I searched in panic. There it was! I quickly ingested the anti-venom, I mean, Benadryl, and waited anxiously for it to take effect. Other than a lingering and painful welt on the back of my neck, I had somehow survived. The encounter taught me one thing: don't ever make eye contact with a wasp. You'll regret it.

Since I was now fully versed in wasp etiquette, I steered clear whenever I saw a nest, and kept my eyes politely averted. So far, this has served me in good stead. The ground hornets and I, on the other hand, unfortunately have yet to come to a cease-fire agreement.

The chickens were in their enclosed chicken run, and it was time for me to get them rounded up and back into the coop for the night. Spunky the rooster refused to cooperate. He darted back into the far recesses of the run as I pursued him. Suddenly I felt my foot sink deep into a soft section of ground. The rest of the area was hard-packed, so why would this be spongy and soft? As my foot sunk, my keen hearing picked up the telltale deep-bass hum that indicated a disturbed and angry nest of ground hornets. I had managed to destroy their home with one misstep.

Spunky took that moment to run to the opposite end, with me close behind, yelling, "Run, Spunky! It's a damn hornet's nest!" This pronouncement served to puzzle him enough that I was able to scoop him up as I ran past in my flight from the killer bees—hornets—whatever. I was quick enough for once that they didn't have the time to marshal their forces and mount a counterattack. I got away that time with no casualties.

Another day, another walk up to the chicken coop. Almost there, a hornet somehow flew up my pant leg, which I didn't realize until it stung me on the upper thigh. I tried to smash it, and was rewarded for my efforts by another sting, this time to my calf. Then another sting, this time to my other calf. I was under full-scale attack.

Running across the yard, I pulled off clothes as I fled. Off came my pants, and a few steps farther, my shirt. I left the clothes where they lay, and sprinted to the house. I was down to my bra and underwear by the time I made it. It's a damn good thing my house is set back into the woods, and the neighbors aren't able to see the goings-on—although I'm sure they have no problem hearing them. As I ran and shed clothing, I swore loudly while swatting at the hornets.

Safe in the house, I took the requisite Benadryl tablet, and made a paste of baking soda to apply to the stings. I scraped off several of the stingers that I could reach. And the sting in my upper thigh? Au contraire. No, it had stung me just a bit higher, in my, shall we say, *nether regions*, and oh my god, was that painful.

After ministering to my wounds, I made a cup of tea and sat carefully and painfully on the front step. A large animal of some type crashed through the woods thirty feet away. I'm not sure if it was a deer, a coyote, the bobcat, or the bear. I didn't much care either. Come and get me, vermin. You can't do much more to me than those hornet bastards have already done.

Afterword

Thinking back over the last thirteen years of utter mayhem since I moved back here to my childhood home, I'm seized of the thought, *What could possibly happen next?* Closely followed by, *What am I still doing here?* Because something invariably does happen next—some type of adrenaline-charging, character-building, grey-hair-inducing something. Things have been relatively quiet as of late, and I suspect some new type of stuff might be about to hit the hobby farm fan.

It's winter once again, and the snow is merely ankle-deep at this juncture, which makes it a delight to traipse through on my daily feeding runs to the chicken coop and the minis' abode. That could change at any moment, of course, and I may soon be flailing through chest-high drifts of the white stuff.

The only bits of excitement in the last few weeks have been the squirrels climbing the cedar siding of the house on their way to leaping onto the bird feeders. They've lately taken to popping up unexpectedly, putting their furry faces right up against the window glass, and staring in at us. Scares the heck out of the cats and dogs—I think that's the point. Breezy goes nuts because she can't get the furry little bastards, and I'd swear one squirrel sticks out his tongue at her and says, "Nyah, nah. You can't get me!" and laughs maniacally as he scampers off up a tree.

The coyotes have been scarce, which is a good thing, and it's a nice change not to hear any howling lately. But knowing them, they're marshaling their vast forces and plotting for a full and final overthrow of my little piece of heaven. I wouldn't put it past those mangy suckers, either.

Dive-bombing hummingbirds. Strafing turkey vultures. Marauding coyotes. Ground hornet strike forces. Livestock dropping dead left and right. And now there are squirrels peeking in at us, taunting us unmercifully, day after day.

On several occasions as I was mopping up after the latest bit of chaos, my brother stopped by, listened to my complaining about all of it, and offered these sage words, "Maybe you should move into an apartment." I'd never tell him this, but he might have a point—or as we say in Minnesota, "Yah, you betcha'."

www.ingramcontent.com/pod-product-compliance
Lightning Source LLC
Chambersburg PA
CBHW072046290426
44110CB00014B/1576